From the Unexpected to Tranquility...

Memories of an Ecumenical Civil Servant

Hans W. Florin

Kirk House Publishers
Minneapolis, Minnesota

From the Unexpected to Tranquility...
Memories of an Ecumenical Civil Servant

Hans W. Florin

Copyright 2012 Hans W. Florin. All rights reserved.

ISBN - 13: 978-1-933794-67-9
ISBN - 10: 1-933794-67-4

Kirk House Publishers, PO Box 390759, Minneapolis, MN 554539
Manufactured in the United States of America

Dedication

To the memory of my friend,
the Rev. Dr. Allan Jenkins,
and
to my grandchildren,
Adeline Marie and Marcus Benjamin

Contents

Foreword 5
Early Years 7
The Path through Parish to Geneva 12
Geneva 22
Africa 30
South Africa 34
Hamburg 45
London 63
    World Association for Christian Communication
    1976-1986 63
    United Bible Societies – Regional Secretary
    of Europe and the Near East 1986-1991 79
Farewell to a Hurried Life 98
A New Chapter 101
Reflecting on the Past 104
Appendix (Acronyms) 106
Chronology 109
Index 111

Foreword

It was my good fortune during my working years in The Lutheran World Federation to be surrounded by colleagues and associates of distinction both in ability and in the capacity for friendship. Among them was the man who has written these memoirs, Hans Florin. He came to Geneva in 1960, with a new doctorate and a new American wife, newly ordained in West Germany, to be my associate. What he really had wanted was Africa, not a European desk job. He had not long to wait. Three years later he got to Africa, but it was South Africa on a special study assignment. He was to look into the divided state of Lutheranism in that *apartheid*-tormented country and suggest what might be done to bring unity and health. One result of his courageous and forthright report was that for the next nineteen years he was unable to get an entry visa to South Africa. Lutherans still have not completed the process of inter-racial consolidation that he argued so strongly for.

Florin was next called back to Germany and, from a base in Hamburg, worked for several years on the modernization and restructuring of the German world missionary movement. Traditionally the program had been carried by voluntary special interest societies; now the national and regional church structures were willing and able to take on the world mission as part of their mandate. There were international implications, and Florin's involvement led to the leadership of an international organization, based then in London and now in Toronto: the World Association for Christian Communication. And that led in time to responsibility for direction of the European regional division of the United Bible Societies.

These pages are not a short history of some structures within the ecumenical movement. They are the memories of one "ecumenical civil servant." But because Hans Florin moved widely among the many and interlocking segments his story cannot fail to illuminate—however sketchily—the fascinating history of the modern world church. That is one reason to read it.

Another is simply to enjoy an account of his years by an energetic, outspoken, forward-looking, and unassuming man who devoted his life to the Christian world mission.

Rev. Dr. Arne Sovik
Minneapolis, Minnesota
August 2012

Early Years

Life is full of memories: tender childhood play-time, an unspoiled fascination with uniformed parades, kindergarten discoveries of the difference between boys and girls (I grew up with two brothers but no sister), school friendships, and a steady expansion of turbulent impressions into many-layered memories of life! It is only later in life—perhaps around 80, when details fade and missed opportunities come to the fore again—that certain focal points surface out of a murky memory-pond around which a skeleton of life experience might be put together. One such focal point was a day in May 1945: Under a blue sky and on the hard-baked clay soil of the American Prisoner of War (POW) Camp Bibelsheim near Bad Kreuznach sat a sixteen- year-old boy in a worn-out Flackhelfer uniform denoting an ex-member of what was known as Luftwaffenhelfer (LWH), also known as Hitler's last hope or more appropriately one of Germany's radar babies. I remember this day well because I had returned to my New Testament, Mark 1:14f: "After John had been arrested, Jesus came into Galilee proclaiming the Gospel of God. 'The time has come; the Kingdom of God is upon you; repent and believe the Gospel!'" With this text came back the memory of a religious education teacher at the Wilhelm Doerpfeld Gymnasium in Wuppertal, who in 1942 told us that with these words Jesus had started his mission and had set the goal of his ministry.

In the POW camp I was aware that the war had come to an end and that Hitler's Third Reich had completely collapsed. Only two months earlier, during the full moon watch of 2:00 to 4:00 a.m., an elderly Swabian corporal and

I walked around our 88-battery in Torgau, carbines firmly slung over our shoulders. We were convinced that the war was lost. During the months before, my LWH buddies and I —most of us kids of pastors of the Confessing Church— had become convinced that Hitler's Germany must be destroyed for the Europe of the Christian West to have a chance to survive.

This knowledge had its first seed some four years earlier (during one of our Saturday afternoon drills) when, in 1941 as a conscripted twelve-year-old *Jungvolk* (pre-Hitler Youth) kid I was selected to the lowest rank of *Jungenschaftsfuehrer* (pre-Hitler Youth squad leader). My father, a pastor of the Confessing Church, helped me decide between 10:00 Sunday mornings "squad leader meetings" and church services. His simple explanation for a twelve year old was that Adolf Hitler was not the Lord Jesus Christ for Germany. Therefore, on Sunday morning I returned the little red and white leader medallion (intertwined red and white string that hung on the uniform tunic between the left breast pocket and center front buttons to symbolize this lowest rank leadership in the pre-Hitler Youth/*Jugend*)!

Only from a post-World War II perspective can one understand the significance of this step. In 1937, after a visit to our home of two Gestapo (secret state police) officials, the Confessing Church thought it wise to suspend my father's chaplaincy at the school, the head of which was a convinced Nazi-Christian. The opposing views of chaplain and director had become publically obvious.

We moved to Wuppertal where my father became the head of the Rhenish Mission Seminary. However, the Gestapo visit in Guetersloh prior to our move to Wuppertal merits further explanation. The personnel file with which the Gestapo had confronted my father was that of a distant cousin with the same name and birthdate—but a different occupation. He was a German Communist Party (DKP) member of parliament of the pre-1933 Weimar Republic. Even Gestapo officials could understand that between 1933 and 1937 a communist politician could not metamorphose into a Confessing Church Lutheran pastor. The cousin was by that time in Moscow.

In May 1945 I was not yet conscious of this. I only remembered that the Gestapo had come once more when, in 1944, my father was already terminally ill in the hospital with pancreatic cancer. On that day in May, in the POW camp, I began to change my mind toward thinking that I might follow my father, who had died on New Year's Eve 1944, into the ministry.

In late August 1945 I came home to the Holy Mountain (location of the Rhenish Mission Seminary) in Wuppertal. My mother had seen me last in Berleburg at my father's funeral. She had to struggle to recognize her son in what she saw: an emaciated, filthy young man with outgrown hair and—as a caution from my side—lice! After her shock, *Mutti* (mother) quickly recovered her authority over her boy: Get out of that dirty uniform and dump it in the rain barrel, she ordered. After a bath, the first in five months, I got into my boy's clothing which had shrunk lengthwise since I had last been in them. And, what was worse, I was ordered to go down the mountain for a haircut: On the way back, she said, stop at Mrs Schaeffer's and ask whether you can get some of Karl-Ludwig's shirts and trousers. Karl-Ludwig—one of my longtime friends, who had a fantastic train set—had not yet come home from the war. He was with the elite "Herman Goering" regiment and had been on a commando mission by U-boat to Scotland to blow up a radar station. Long after the war, when we lived in England, Karl-Ludwig, who loved his Mercedes, did not dare drive it to our home for a visit because "the Brits may still be interested in getting hold of me." In my office hangs a glass dolphin transparency as a thank you for a lecture I gave in the early 1970s in Germany to a group of his friends on Bible work in Eastern Europe.

One of the first things this POW had to face was going back to school. Not long after my mother moved back to Guetersloh in 1946, I continued my education at the same grammar school (Das Evangelisch-Stiftische Gymnasium—ESG) where my father had been chaplain before the war.

After graduation from school and studying theology at Heidelberg, Gottingen, and Muenster, I was awarded a World Council of Churches (WCC) scholarship to Colgate Rochester Divinity School (CRDS) in upstate New York. I disembarked in Quebec, Canada, from a converted liberty ship designed to transport immigrants. I was very fortunate to have been given the opportunity to attend the Second Assembly of the WCC in Evanston, Illinois, in mid-1954. The WCC, first fully installed in 1948 in Amsterdam, was still a novelty. So was the enthusiastic hope for worldwide realized Christian unity.

The WCC Assembly was held on the campus of Northwestern University. There one crossed paths with non-Catholic church leaders whose names and robes were strange: Orthodox, Armenian, Coptic, Syriac, and more—for me at best signals from distant recesses of church history. The one church and ecumenical leader who left a lasting impression on me was the Right Reverend George Allan Kennedy Bell, (Anglican) bishop of Chichester and chairman of the WCC Central Committee. Little did I know then that I would later have the privilege of working in three ecumenical organizations, the formation of which owe their existence to Bishop Bell's influence and help: the WCC, The World Association of Christian Communication (WACC), and the United Bible Societies (UBS).

After the WCC Assembly in 1954, I came with many as yet undigested impressions to the peaceful and spacious campus of Colgate Rochester Divinity School (CRDS). For a twenty-six year old, less than ten years after the massive destruction of Germany in WW II, America was indeed an overpowering experience!

The three formative impulses from my time at CRDS were:

1. My first experience of the ecumenical reality of U.S. Christianity. CRDS was a well-reputed, liberal Baptist seminary. Its student body and faculty came from a number

of other denominations: Congregational, Presbyterian, Methodist, and more. As a German Lutheran I was a happily tolerated exotic exception.

2. For the WCC scholarship year I had requested to study the field of sociology of religion. In Prof. Albert T. Rasmussen, CRDS had a well-reputed teacher on this topic. This man formed my outlook on a wide range of institutional realities in Christendom. Especially fascinating became the insight into the differing socio-political strata of American denominations—from upper-class Episcopalians to several diversified middle-class levels of Methodists, Presbyterians, Congregationalists, and Baptists (north, south, and exclusive). Roman Catholics were widely identified by their immigrant backgrounds: Irish, Italian, Hispanic; Lutherans by their Scandinavian and German roots. This widely differing world of American Christianity tempted me to design a denominational slide-rule from which one could glean social, political, economic, and ethnic preferences. Needless to say, this idea remained an unfulfilled temptation.

3. My American language usage improved and prospered greatly. On arriving in the Western hemisphere my English was practically non-existent. That I slithered through the WCC-scholarship suitability test I owe mostly to my absorption of the American Forces Network (AFN) lingo in Heidelberg (1950-1952). My grammar school (1939-1949) language study started with Latin, followed by Greek and French, and finished with English.

Living with students and faculty on the hill helped my orientation in the extraordinarily vibrant world of post-World War II U.S.A. But more lasting than this learning curve turned out to be a more natural event: I fell in love with the research assistant of the director of the CRDS field work department, Dorothy Wilder, my future wife of forty-six years.

Looking back over these focal points of my formative years, I realize that the switch points for my ecumenical and international ministry were set. It prepared me for much of what followed after 1955.

The Path through Parish to Geneva

I can't remember when my mind was drawn to Africa. Early pictures included animals, the likes of which were certainly not part of my childhood—elephants, lions, giraffes, zebras, and more—but most of all I remember that the people who lived in Africa were black. That such a mysterious Africa should become a part of my working life emerged only later.

When I returned to Germany in late 1955 I had to follow the next steps of the non-academic training for the ministry: assistance in parish work, further course work for a yet to be defined specialized qualification and, of course, practical preparation for pastoral care, worship, and the basics of administrating the sacraments of baptism and communion. During a brief visit to my New Testament professor at Muenster, the idea of doctoral studies in the options of general ministry came up. Should it be in diaconal services or in mission? My father, prior to his early death, had been the head of the Rhenish Mission Seminary and, during the war, pastor of a parish in Wuppertal; my choice was mission.

The natural next step was to be a course at the Mission Academy in Hamburg. However, prior to such specialized training there had to be a period of assistance in parish work. My posting as synod assistant was to Superintendent Steinsiek in Hagen at the eastern edge of the Ruhr. I could not have had a better or wiser teacher! Sermons, liturgy, and Sunday school became my regular activities. I will never forget my first two funerals: the first for a prominent member of the Communist Party in Hagen and shortly thereafter for a football player from one of the Hagen clubs. Without Superintendent Steinsiek I would have panicked: I cannot do funerals! Can't you please do them? No, and no again. Superintendent Steinsiek had been in a Nazi concentration camp with the Communist. They knew each other well. Any pastoral word from the superintendent would be carefully weighed, analyzed, and also likely mischievously exploited. But what should I do? Superintendent Steinsiek reminded me: You preach the Gospel of our Lord Jesus Christ—that is what my Communist friend needs. The footballer funeral was quite a different challenge. During the service there were no other words than liturgy; after the blessing of the coffin at the grave other comments could be made. But how does one keep calm, cool, and collected for later comments when the team's football is dropped into the grave and bounced happily on the casket, followed by shock-stricken, almost inaudible words from his team mates?

My time with Superintendent Steinsiek remains the most wholesome experience of my practical training, and he participated in my ordination in November 1960.

The Hamburg Mission Academy was at its beginning in 1956. Hamburg was the seat of the German Mission Council, the umbrella organisation of some forty to fifty separate and independent mission societies. The first crop of students, mostly pre-ordination theologians, lived in Alsterdorf, a handicap institute of the Lutheran Church of Hamburg. From Alsterdorf one reached the Mission Council on Mittelweg via tram line No. 9 after about twelve stops. One reached the airport by only two stops.

The lectures at the council were mostly carried by the two council leaders, Freytag and Hermelink, whose outlooks on the world were necessarily shaped by pre-war visits in the culturally and geographically widely divergent German mission fields. Not only had one prominent Berlin missionary been the Nazi *Ortsgruppenleiter* (area group leader) of Dar es Salaam, but the German Mission Council would not sign the Confession of Guilt Declaration of the German EKD member churches in the autumn of 1945. In this context I did not find much inspiration at the Mission Academy. More interesting were the job opportunities at Hamburg Airport: I worked as traffic agent at Icelandic Airlines and twice weekly as night manager for Seaboard and Western Airlines, a freight carrier.

This latter job entailed a rather noisy surprise. A freight feeder DC3 from Ireland with American cargo for northern Germany landed at 3:00 a.m. One item on the bill of lading was a dog, to be transferred to the first Lufthansa flight to Bremen. Yes, there was a dog—a little pooch, very thirsty, that hastily licked from every tarmac water puddle on the way to the office. After dispatching the cargo for overland transport, I delivered the dog to Lufthansa. On returning to the office, I not only found a healthy piddle pool on the office floor, but within the hour I had the liveliest telephone call from a U.S. Army captain from Bremer Haven, then still an American enclave in North Germany. The language was harsh and blue, angry beyond belief, and definitely unfit for print. What I could make out in the end was that this captain expected his beloved and long-missed German shepherd to be delivered to him instead of this tiny excuse for a real dog. After some telex and phone calls I discovered that the dogs were mixed up in Ireland, and the German shepherd was already back on his way to the U.S.A. I never heard of this story again or if Seaboard and Western faced a claim for compensation.

What challenge there was at the Mission Academy consisted of sound lectures in sociology at Hamburg University. Prof. Karl Heinz Pfeffer was for me as influential as Albert T. Rasmussen of Colgate Rochester Divinity School. Pfeffer was a wonderful matter-of-fact teacher and later the head of the World Economic Archive in Kiel. His lectures were brilliant political and economic overviews of an Africa at the threshold of independence. I owe it to this man that Africa became the focal point for my next life experiences.

(It was the wish of the Pfeffer family that, if available, I should bury my esteemed teacher. A bit over a decade later I buried Professor Pfeffer in the graveyard of the Hessian village of his birth—my way of thanking this exceptional teacher.)

During my time with him, Prof. Pfeffer quickly realized that the Mission Academy would not be useful for my further studies, nor would the Africa Department of Hamburg University. In his opinion there were only three African study centers worth considering: one in the United Kingdom, the School of Oriental and African Studies (SOAS) of London University; and two in the USA: Northwestern University in Illinois or the African Research and Studies Program (ARSP) at Boston University. But how would one pick the right one?

Like so often in my life another unforeseen circumstance came up. As a result of my jobbing at Hamburg Airport, Icelandic Air offered me a ten percent round-trip ticket (Hamburg-New York City-Hamburg) for the 1956 Christmas break. I shall not forget my interview with Dr Brown, the director of ARSP in Boston. During World War II Dr Brown had been the head of the Africa section of the U.S. Department of State. Yes, I would be qualified for a Ph.D. program at Boston University. And yes, there would be a scholarship from the Ford Foundation, which funded ARSP. But, in light of my theology background, I should pro-forma register at the Boston University Divinity School for ecumenical studies with Prof. Nils Ehrenstrom, the retired secretary of the World Council of Churches Studies Department in Geneva.

The start for my Ph.D. program was set for autumn 1957, after our marriage on 21 September 1957 in Sacramento, California. Through Dorothy's Baptist connections there was a position for her administering the personnel and pension files of Baptist ministers in New England. with an office in Tremont Temple in Boston. Thus, both our living and my academic costs were covered until graduation in June 1960.

The arrival in Boston was less traumatic than my lone entry to CRDS in Rochester, New York, in 1954. The ARSP was slightly east of the Boston University (BU) campus, in its own house directly on the south bank of the Charles River. This location had the dual advantage that the BU lecture theaters were only a five-minute walk away and the delightful summer Boston Pops outdoor concerts were some ten minutes along the river to the east.

The immediate ambience of ARSP was simply beyond any academic comparison: eleven professors and twenty-seven students together in one building. Each student had a desk and each professor had an office, the doors of which were always open. The commons room had room for all, plus the frequent visitors from Africa. The emerging political leadership of the soon-to-be independent nations were usually sent by the U.S. Department of State to Boston University. The sessions with leaders such as Kwame Nkrumah of Ghana or Julius Nyerere of Tanzania were unforgettable.

I can still see the faces of these leaders. The years of indignity and humiliation had left traces of hardship in their features, along with determination and readiness to liberate their people from colonial suppression. With them Africa would change! But could we, a post-colonial Europe, recognize and accept this change?

With our own desks we mostly treated the house of ARSP as our office building. We kept hours—9:00 a.m. to 5:00 p.m. or later was customary. Our contacts with our lecture tutors were frequent and uncomplicated. The atmosphere in the house was happy. Seminar sessions were free. Lecture topics and reports covered anthropology, economics, and politics. The ARSP orientation was liberal—befitting the general liberal outlook of the Boston academic scene of Harvard and Massachusetts Institute of Technology (MIT). Our assignments were probing; superficial papers were unacceptable.

I remember one tutelage about the ethnic structure of the Nuer, a tribe in the Upper Nile of Sudan, a region they shared with their neighbors, the Dinka. Both groups raided their territories in pursuit of cattle, necessary for showing off one's traditional wealth, creating a mutually hostile environment. In the late 1950s the standard work about the Nuer was by an Italian Roman Catholic missionary priest who had discovered that the Nuer traced their ancestry and beginnings to 1923 and the then still existing tree of life. What community could be further removed from post-World War II reality than the Nuer? Within weeks of that discovery, in an inter-university student group, I met a Nuer Ph.D. student from MIT. A greater trans-historic and inter-cultural jump did not seem imaginable!

Quite unique within this tightly knit structure of ARSP was my relationship with Prof. Nils Ehrenstrom, a Swede. He was accessible by booking a meeting. His office, with happy cigar aroma, was packed with books, piles of papers, and reports, as well as an enormous and also enviably complex card index. Any ecumenical paper, thought, or conference could be retrieved immediately. But it took Nils Ehrenstrom's personal memory and knowledge to put all this information into its proper context. Ehrenstrom knew all the ecumenical leaders personally. He remembered clearly the pre-1945 contacts with the German churches, which were not always easy. He knew and appreciated my heroes, George Bell and Dietrich Bonhoeffer. His tutelage made my unexpected entry into Geneva pleasantly easy. After his retirement Ehrenstom settled in Switzerland, close to Geneva, where I had the opportunity to see him for a last time. It was only in later years that I realized how much of my formation I owed to Nils Ehrenstrom.

After my June 1960 graduation we moved to Germany—a first for my American wife Dorothy! There I was needed to complete one more professional exam as well as take on the responsibility for a 7,000-soul congregation in Guetersloh-East. This parish was preparing to be divided into a rural and a suburban part. In addition to all pastoral care, worship services, religious instruction—which started with 27 hours per week—one of my tasks was to organize the parish's preparation for division. This meant meetings with the elders, review of applications and setting up a schedule for test services for the selected candidates to serve the parish. Particularly the rural elder, a sturdy farmer, was worried that I might not be up to all this. I failed the "belonging test" because I was not baptized with Dalke water, a little river running through the local extended farm land. Only after I told him that I had grown up in Guetersloh and had graduated from the local grammar school, where my father had been chaplain before the war, did the elder feel all right. He determined he could work with this newly baked pastor—and work we did indeed. Without this man the division of the parish would not have come off like clockwork.

My ordination as Lutheran pastor of the Church in Westphalia fell in the midst of all this activity. I was ordained on 11 November 1960 in my little rural parish church, St. Mark, by Heinrich Lohmann, superintendent of the Guetersloh district, assisted by *Superintendent im Ruhestand* (superintendent in retirement) Steinsiek and my godfather, Dean Wilhelm Brandt, who in passing mentioned that through his participation in the ordination blessing I was bestowed the apostolic succession. Had I taken this latter gift more seriously, my later services in the ecumenical and the Anglican world might have been easier.

My time in Guetersloh was short. My memories are few. My local superintendent, Heinrich Lohmann, understood immediately that twenty-seven weekly hours of religious instruction in schools and parish was too much. Within days he had a curate for me, ordained and with more experience than I had. This man was a vibrant extrovert, looking desperately for a wife. His sister, a Lufthansa flight attendant, tried to be helpful. On occasions my curate drove to Frankfurt for cabin crew parties. At 2:00 p.m. on the day I turned in my parish seal and registers, he called to say he was stuck on the *autobahn*; could I please take the funeral at 2:30 p.m.—and no, he didn't know the name of the deceased. I had thirty minutes. With Superintendent

Steinsiek's advice I just about managed, but I was angry when I learned later that I had buried an elderly lady whom I had visited in a care home a couple of times.

Another memorable Guetersloh funeral occurred in the spring of 1961. Three weeks after I had buried a well-known farmer, his wife died. She had told me on her sickbed that she had wanted to die first to prepare for her husband one of the mansions which the Lord Jesus had told us he had ready for those who believe. It was clear that this lady, a faithful member of the parish's women's aid group, was not happy with her Heavenly Father.

Her funeral was a massive affair: Busloads of farming folk filled the graveyard chapel. Our organist, highly qualified, with her own recordings on the market, liked to modify the melody line of each verse. In addition, her modern chords made the hymns unsingable. This irritated my farmer congregation. Although the dead farmer's widow might have been annoyed by that, what was to follow might have been even more alarming.

It was always the custom that six gentlemen from a care home nearby should be available for funeral duty. On that day I had the last service. Winter rain had softened Guetersloh's sandy soil. When I followed the six coffin bearers to the grave, they already had a rather unsteady gait. At the grave side this proved to be too much: one of them, in order to steady himself, stepped back onto the grave's edge. The inevitable happened. The edge gave way, and this man slid with a lot of sand into the grave and under the casket still resting above the grave. "Get me out, damn it, get me out" could be heard by the grandsons of the deceased, carrying wreaths. Without a word they parked the wreaths, pulled the chap out, dusted him off, and the service came to a good end.

After I left the parish I often pondered whether the organist ever had learned to muster appropriate empathy with the bereaved, and whether the public graveyard administration might have changed the custom of a case of beer for each funeral.

In the early spring of 1961 the test services for the candidates at St. Mark's parish allowed us time for our first and long promised trip in Europe—to Geneva, Rome, and Athens. In Geneva, the seat of the WCC, I met with Bishop Lesslie Newbigin about an ecumenical placement anywhere in Africa—except South Africa. As Newbigin had no immediate offer, a friend suggested that I talk to Dr Arne Sovik, director of the Lutheran World Federation (LWF) Department of World Mission. Dr Sovik needed an assistant director in his department, but I wanted something in Africa—and anyway, we first wanted to finish our European trip.

In Rome we visited one of Dorothy's cousins, married to a Baptist missionary to the Romans. But this contradiction-in-terms encounter did not deter us from seeing the Vatican, St. Peter's Basilica, and the Gardens. From Brindisi we took a ferry to Piraeus, the port to Athens. For a humanist grammar school student (with Latin and Greek), Athens had long been the crowning location of a long anticipated pilgrimage. As it was only early spring in Greece, there were not many tourists. The Acropolis, then still freely accessible, was and remains a unique experience. Among the few tourists, a young Italian lady tried to negotiate the rubble field in slender high-heeled red shoes. Definitely not recommended! The Agora, the center of the ancient city state, brought up the memory of the philosophers of olden times, who meditated and debated the principles and values for what is right for succeeding communities, from which Europe emerged. On Mars Hill, from which classic Greek justice was dispensed and where, according to tradition, St. Paul addressed the Athenians, we celebrated together with the small German expatriate congregation the Easter morning service of the Roman calendar. Orthodox Easter was to be a week later.

At Delphi, where Pythia, the most renowned priestess of Apollo, pronounced her oracles, much in demand in the ancient world, we came across a Greek National Ballet dancer. Thanks to his fluent English we learned that the standard Greek Easter dish was roasted lamb. This charming young man sat in front of his parents' house, overlooking the Isthmus of Corinth, and cleaned a freshly slaughtered lamb for his family's Easter banquet. His invitation to stay and celebrate Easter with his clan was a big temptation. Alas, we had to catch our ferry back to Italy.

On the bus trip down Mount Parnassus we stopped at Hosios Loukas, the Orthodox monastery. As luck would have it, we met an old grey-bearded monk, quietly looking over a wall into a wide range of hills and valleys. As we stood next to him, sharing his view, we learned that he was from the Bronx, New York. He was a retired monk, awaiting his release into the holy eternity of this wonderful monastery. Yet, prior to his end, he expected to be part of the monastery's Easter celebration. He showed us the faintly lit pre-Easter church, the chapels, library, and refectory. From his anticipation we could imagine to what light and glory all this would arise on Easter morning.

Back in Brindisi we picked up our old Fiat Mille Cento and headed north: Venice, Vienna, Luxembourg (where the road maps are calibrated in 200-meter slots), Belgium, and Holland.

In Guetersloh telegrams and phone calls from Geneva awaited us. "When are you coming? How do you want to appear on the letterhead?" I called Arne Sovik and told him that I had not yet been in touch with my *Landeskirchenamt* (church headquarters) and my president. Arne's short response: "I have done that. Your *Praeses* (president) Dr. Thimme wants you to be in Geneva rather than somewhere in Africa. So, when are you coming? The sooner the better!"

Geneva

We arrived in Geneva on 2 May 1961 and took over a simple studio flat in Avenue Krieg. The Lutheran World Federation (LWF) on the ecumenical campus on Route de Malagnou was a different world. There were international staff, daily contact with extended parts of the world, and gathering and organizing masses of information for the annual meeting of the LWF Commission for World Mission (CWM), which this year was scheduled for the last week of July. Arne Sovik put me in the hands of Lilo Schiller, a wise and experienced secretary, whom Bishop Hanns Lilje of Hanover, a former LWF president, had bestowed on the LWF. All preparation had to be in place for the CWM conference at the end of July in Berlin. Did I have the feeling of jumping into the deep end of this new world? You bet! Had it not been for Lilo Schiller I might have drowned.

A big part of the planning was preparation of the one-inch thick conference book—containing a detailed annotated agenda, the outlines for daily worship, a list for funding requests for action by CWM, and an extensive description of projects, analyses, budgets, and suggested funding proposals. With a couple of Lilo's younger colleagues from the LWF World Service department, we developed a format of project presentation which later became the standard for use by mission, diaconal world service, scholarships, and development undertakings. From the LWF this format spread to the parallel World Council of Churches departments and to the aid agencies of the German churches. A significant contribution by Arne Sovik in this procedure was a suggested text for each anticipated

CWM action. At conference, however, the chairman of CWM, Bishop Heinrich Meyer of Luebeck, felt free to alter any proposals after discussion in plenary or in regional committees.

When we reviewed the agenda with Bishop Meyer prior to the Berlin meeting, I learned that directly following the CWM conference, Dr. Sovik and his family would depart from Berlin for a three-month sabbatical in the U.S.A., and I would be serving as interim head of the department. And if that wasn't enough, could I please also do the opening address at the conference? Arne's advice for the address was simple: Say something of where you come from and where you think mission should go. Whenever I felt like I was drowning in those early days of swimming in unfamiliar waters, Lilo Schiller became my dependable life jacket.

By way of introduction, I told the conference of my African studies in Boston and having met some of the up-and-coming leaders of the soon-to-be independent nations. I suggested that, as we at CWM represented different German, American, and Scandinavian mission fields, it was not unrealistic to anticipate independent indigenous churches and to integrate them within a nation or culture of the various western mission fields.

There wasn't much response from the mission bosses present in Berlin—except from Dr. Gerhard Brennecke, the head of the Berlin Mission. He thanked me as a man of perspectives similar to his own. While in Berlin, CWM was bussed to the Berlin Mission headquarters twice for visits in East Berlin. Little could any of us have known that some three weeks after the conference, the wall would go up in Berlin, separating East from West. In later years I visited Dr. Brennecke a couple of times, especially at the fortnightly staff meetings of the then still united Evangelical Church of Germany (EKD). In the morning we met in West Berlin, with the afternoon meeting in East Berlin. Germans had to pass through the underground stop *Friedrichstrasse*. Non-Germans went above ground through Checkpoint Charlie. Neither route was always an easy border crossing.

After the CWM conference there was an officers and staff dinner at an upstairs Chinese restaurant close to Kaiser Wilhelm Memorial Church. Circulating with pre-dinner drinks in hand and reliving unminuted tidbits from the conference, one of us noticed that Arne Sovik was missing. Of course, as an old China hand he discussed the dinner and its options with the chef in the kitchen—naturally in Chinese. The meal was delicious, the goodbyes warm and grateful, and the minutes were left in the hands of Arne's extremely capable Swiss secretary Elsbeth.

Back in Geneva, a less hectic day-to-day schedule allowed me to explore structural details of the LWF and especially of the far more extensive WCC. It was not difficult to discover that, as far as policy was concerned, there was not much difference between the ecumenical WCC Department of Inter-Church Aid, Refugees and World Service (WCC DICARWS) and the LWF Department of World Service (LWF WS)—both shared the Good Samaritan concern for the poor and disadvantaged, which in those years included refugees.

The LWF World Service department operated a Palestinian refugee camp near Jericho. As a result of the 1948 war between the Arab League with Jordan and Israel, many Palestinians lost their homes, land, and freedom. Besides the Jericho camp, LWF WS also ran the Augusta Victoria Hospital, a pre-World War I foundation of Germany's Kaiser Wilhelm II, as a depot for food aid and equipment for emergency assistance.

Also the fundraising technique was similar, using government contributions where possible as well as widely distributed public appeals with emotionally loaded visual aids—pictures, video clips, and exhibitions. Both fiscal support and returns from public appeals depended on rather graphic illustrations of need, together with the assurance that the administration of the funds would remain in professional (that is, Western) hands. It is not difficult to grasp that there was room for competitive tension between fundraising for mission and for diaconal service projects.

After the Berlin CWM conference there emerged one sizeable project which would become part of both, mission and service—a modern multi-ward teaching hospital in Moshi, Tanzania. That it was on the CWM agenda was no coincidence: Mission hospitals have a long and well-respected tradition in world mission! Through medical mission hospitals, doctors, and nurses, much suffering in the mission fields has been treated and life improved.

Detailed plans or costs for the Moshi project had not yet been available when on 18 September 1961 the world was shocked by the air crash and death in northeast Africa of Dag Hammarskjöld, the U.N. general secretary. September 18 was also a day on which all senior LWF staff were at a retreat, away from the office. I was the ranking staff at the LWF premises when the telephone rang, long distance from Sweden. Åke Kastlund, general director of Kirkens Noedhelp in Uppsala, offered to go on national television that evening and raise all the money we would need for the hospital—one, two, or more million U.S. dollars—if I could confirm that this project would be called the Dag Hammarskjöld Memorial Hospital. I must admit that my feathers got a bit ruffled—who is Kastlund, what is Kirkens Noedhelp? No, we have no name yet, and no, I can't ask anybody else, but I will check with the CWM chairman, Bishop Heinrich Meyer, in Luebeck. A bit condescendingly Kastlund agreed: "OK, you do that—but I must have a reply within the hour, one-and-a-half hours at the latest, or no public appeal on Swedish national television!"

Heinrich Meyer, himself a former missionary in India, said something like: "Isn't that typical, for money we should decide *that* name for an *African* hospital? Tell Åke Kastlund that in due course we will ask our friends in Africa through Bishop Moshi." Naturally, Åke Kastlund was very unhappy! When I put the phone down after my call to Kastlund, I still had Åke's not exactly quiet words ringing in my ear: "Wrong choice, poor leadership; you will hear more of this!"

And more I did hear after the retreat. The Australian director of the LWF WS simply could not understand why I gratefully did not accept Kastlund's generous offer: "Indeed, that does look like poor leadership, and Arne Sovik will hear of this!"

After the dust had settled I began to realise that my "lack of leadership" had prevented one of the most powerful men behind LWF WS from highjacking the Moshi project away from CWM. Today I still smile about this.

Another day in post-conference wrap-up went like this: Through the door of my office came an imposing, tall man in black vest and dog collar. He pulled out the chair in front of my desk and sat down: "So, you are Hans Florin."

I had no idea who that guy was. "May I enquire who you are?"

There was quite an amazed face across my desk, and a soft, friendly smile: "Of course, why should you know, being so new here? I am Franklin Clark Fry, president of the LWF, of the Lutheran Church in America (LCA), and chairman of the WCC Central and Executive Committees. Every fortnight or so I come here to check that everything goes well."

We had an interesting discussion about the world, the ecumenical scene, and some good advice for my future in this august environment. Lilo Schiller laughed and could not believe that I had not heard of Franklin Clark Fry. Over the years Fry and I got to know each other better. And today I am still in awe of this highly intelligent and powerful man.

After Arne Sovik's return, my travelling days slowly began to take shape: visiting mission societies and LWF member churches, asking for help and contributions for the CWM project budget. CWM's wide ranging constituency came slowly into focus.

During this time there occurred an interregnum in the English-speaking part of the Lutheran church in Geneva. The American pastor's term had come to an end and a new one had not yet been appointed. The Lutheran church in

Geneva was not far from the beautiful Calvinist Cathedral St. Pierre, in the old part of the city. In contrast to the Calvinist established church, churches of other denominations could not have steeples. Our church in Bourg-de-Four was a small manor house with a sizeable assembly room and a Calvinistically high pulpit on the empty wall behind the altar table. Ordained LWF staff took turns having services during the interregnum.

Once, when it was my Sunday, I recognized Franklin Clark Fry in the congregation. From the pulpit it was clearly visible that this man in the center of the auditorium sat in an otherwise empty circle, left to him out of respect. After the service, at the door, there was an impersonal handshake from the president of the LWF: "Thoughtful sermon, thank you." Later I learned that such a remark from Franklin Clark Fry was not bad.

On occasions when the German organist fell ill, often on short notice, Dorothy had to step in. In her home Baptist church in Medford, Oregon, she often had organ duty. Her repertoire differed somewhat from the standard Geneva fare. Accompanying hymns and providing pitch for the part of the sung liturgy was doable. However, the preludes and postludes were another matter. Hers were softer and closer to a U.S. West Coast style. Once, an American lady from the congregation congratulated her: "I like your pieces, not always Bach and all that jazz." Dorothy took that to be a compliment—"sometimes one has to be grateful for little favors"—and that was typical of Dorothy.

With all my anticipation and intensive preparation for Africa, I thought I should have a chance to see Africa, the continent which had been on my mind for years. However, there was another hurdle for the patience that we—Dorothy especially—had to muster: We had to learn to become parents. On 15 March 1963, some ten days late, our son Marc was born. A last check-up revealed that the birth should best be done by caesarean section.

The maternity hospital was on Route de Malagnou, right across from the office. The caesarean was scheduled for 2:30 p.m. In her wisdom Lilo Schiller had decided that she should go with her inexperienced boss across the street and keep him calm. On the floor above the operation theater there was a special waiting area by the elevator. When 2:30 came, Lilo exercised her calming skills: "Don't fret; it will take a while yet."

Although there was soon a fresh baby cry, Lilo knew this wasn't for us. But almost immediately the crying came closer and louder. The elevator started to rise, stopped, and the door opened. A young nurse in golden slippers pushed a cot out and announced: "*Voila, votre fils!*" I looked at this unwashed bundle of tiny humanity, dumbfounded.

I had to find out from Lilo what this was. "Oh, are you so dense? It is your son. Follow the nurse and watch through the glass door window to see how he will be washed, weighed, measured, and wrapped."

When my feet hit the ground again I learned that the mother was fine and happy. She would now be sown up and allowed to rest. I could see her after 5:00 p.m.—time enough to order the print of the birth announcements and a quick call to Dorothy's parents in Oregon.

I was back in the hospital at 5:00 p.m.—and alone! Dorothy was tired but very happy! She had heard her son's voice from the baby ward. But now she wanted to see him! The gold-slippered nurse rolled him in, asleep. The mother's instruction: "You unwrap him, check his fingers and toes, and let me hold him." I will never forget that serene and happy look on this new mother's face! And all was fine—limbs, neck, head and a sweet breath. I tried to put him together again. This French wrapping was different from what I remembered my mother doing with my brothers who were four and six years younger. The friendly nurse finished the job with a smile.

Supper time approached. Dorothy had heard that the kitchen in this hospital was excellent. However, instead of a medium-well done *entrecote*, the tempting aroma of which came from beyond the door, Dorothy's post-op portion consisted of a cup of tea and dry toast. And as disappointments usually come in pairs, Dorothy began to realize that the happy cry of her son was the croak of a raven outside her window. So much for "I recognized the voice of my child."

As a family we moved into a slightly larger flat in the Rue de 31 Decembre, from the balcony of which one could see the Jet d'Eau in Lake Geneva.

Africa

My first trip to Africa came about within three weeks of son Marc's birth. My first jet flight with a BOAC Comet to Dar Es Salaam was uneventful, except that my luggage did not arrive. It was Easter Saturday; the next flight would come on the Tuesday after Easter. A German missionary we had met in Heidelberg helped out with what I needed in the mean time.

The first night in an African hotel, a red brick building from before World War I *Deutsch Ost-Afrika* (German East Africa) was an adventure. How does one untangle a mosquito net—and what about the many holes in it? The water was murky, neither hot nor cold; the bed a bit lumpy. Nonetheless, it took my tired body aboard for a wonderful and deep sleep, accompanied by the steady noise of crickets.

The first conscious sound the next morning was bare feet on the tiled floor and some shuffling by my bedside table: "Good morning, Bwana. Hot tea." It was barely 6:00 in the morning,

After breakfast, a choice of Cooked English (including smoked kippers) or Continental (stale bread), the German missionary picked me up for the Easter morning services. It was already warm and humid.

My assignment in Tanzania was a visit with Bishop Moshi in Moshi town, a look around where the hospital project might fit in and a visit to Makumira, the seminary for future Lutheran pastors. There was also a German theologian on the faculty. We had met in the Mission Academy in Hamburg.

Bishop Moshi welcomed me as an old friend. We had met in two CWM meetings, and I remembered him from a visit in Geneva when the plans for the Lutheran shortwave station Radio Voice of the Gospel (RVOG) and its location in Ethiopia were discussed. Regarding the Moshi hospital there were no further plans, except to note that it later became known as the Kilimanjaro Mission Hospital. The ideas of the two mission doctors were formidable. The hope of a mission administrator concentrated on something manageable! In the end, the hospital became a substantial regional medical establishment—which in time, as happens so often in Africa, came under government control.

From Makumira Seminary two African phenomena stayed in my mind—the East African Motor Rally and the incredible fertility of the iron-red soil of Africa. Neither phenomenon had anything to do with the seminary.

On the first evening at Makumira, the cooling night air was interrupted by some far-off, non-African, non-animal noise. We became aware that students had drifted down the hill to a sandy trail which represented the main thoroughfare of that part of the country—the highway to Nairobi, Kenya. From the students I learned that the East African Motor Rally would come through that evening—an annual event which one should not miss. And, indeed, it was impressive when out of total darkness first the loom, then the roaring engine noise was followed by the brights of the car lights, signaling the approach of a really fast touring car. What about animals, I wondered, perhaps elephants, on the road? Animals know better I was told—especially on a night like this! Instead, rocks or tree trunks were greater dangers, and they did irreparably damage cars each year. In those years it was usually a Peugeot 404 that won the rally.

The morning after the rally, in the garden of my German faculty host, I saw what I thought was a raw broom stick, with some bark still attached. "Why do you have this broom sticking in the ground?"

He responded, "This is no broom stick! I brought this with me from home. It is an oak branch. I would like to plant a German oak tree in this African soil!" I was informed that there is not much that would *not* grow and flourish in African soil, and perhaps the oak's roots already had sprouted underground. Indeed, a wonderful gift of our Creator God to this beloved continent!

Back in Geneva, life began to grow beyond our accustomed routine. Marc was with us in our flat. We were lucky that because of his sufficient birth weight—some 3400 grams—the maternity ward had him sleep through the night.

In the office things began to change too.

In the summer came two offers to move to Africa—one from the faculty of Makumira Seminary to join them; the other from South Africa, to analyze Lutheran missions in that country and explore structures for integrating the different mission fields into one Evangelical Lutheran Church of South Africa (ELCSA).

The Makumira invitation included the question of whether the candidate was morally up-standing enough for the task. The American Mission Superintendent Ruben Petersen set the seminary board's concerns at rest with the comment that "Dr. Florin smokes an occasional pipe and drinks an occasional glass of beer."

One board member, so I learned later, was heard to have said: "Oh, he must be a very remarkable German." But Makumira did not become my future.

The position in South Africa had been requested by The Lutheran World Federation Commission for World Mission several times before. The various Lutheran mission groups in South Africa repeatedly had asked for an outside analysis of their outlook on mission life and service in separated apartheid South Africa. Not only had the British Commonwealth repealed South Africa's membership, but, parallel to the civil rights struggle in the U.S.A., the world had become increasingly aware of the existing racial tensions in South Africa. From among the major churches in South Africa it seemed that only the Lutheran work there had an ambivalent profile. The Dutch Reformed churches had, through their predominantly Boer membership, a supportive affinity to the apartheid regime. The Anglican and Roman Catholic communions were each—according to the guidance of their respective canon laws—one interracial church. But what was the position of the Lutherans?

After several persons, whom the LWF had suggested for this analysis, had been rejected by the divergent Lutherans factions, the request to try once more had come to Geneva. The Swedish Bishop Helge Fosseus raised the issue again, and Arne Sovik and Bishop Heinrich Meyer proposed that I should have a go at it this time, that my training would have prepared me for doing justice to this task.

For our family this decision had a very mixed appeal. My childhood impressions of South Africa were formed by the Rhenish mission stories from *Deutsch Sued-West Africa* (German Southwest Africa). My adult view of South Africa was critical. What should be my next step?

As a thirty-five year old, I did not feel as old as Jesus' word in John 21:18 would suggest about the destiny of an old man: "But when you are old you will stretch out your arms, and a stranger will bind you fast and carry you where you have no wish to go." This "going where you don't want to go" had been my challenge and orientation throughout my adult life. I had often said "anywhere in Africa, but not South Africa!" So it was to South Africa where the LWF commissioned me to go for two years.

South Africa

It was now the autumn of 1963. Our years in Geneva and with The Lutheran World Federation (LWF) had been exciting: life in a different culture and a different language (French) was fascinating. Daily contacts with colleagues from other countries and other churches wore down political and religious prejudices. And the ecumenical ideal to wish and work for Christian unity—which Jesus Christ himself considered essential for the world to believe (John 17) and with which Calvin's city of Geneva has been so singularly connected—had, of course, a formative influence. Friendships from Geneva days long outlasted the anticipated sense of warm nostalgia for the beautiful city.

The professional preparation for Africa in previous years now slipped somewhat to the background behind the practical planning for the move to South Africa. Marc had to be introduced to his wider families. In May 1963 Marc was baptized in Germany. The long-standing family friend, Hartmut Warns from Guetersloh, whose parish I had briefly looked after prior to Geneva, baptized Marc in Girkhausen im Wittgensteiner Land. That Marc was baptized with Jordan water did not go over all that well with the severe and no-nonsense Calvinist pastor there. However, the parish elder, organist, and Sunday school leader—in light of the fact that my great and great-great grandfather had been pastors of this parish between 1813 and 1887—swept away this concern with this apt remark: "Whenever a Florin gets baptized in the Girkhausen church, the incumbent pastor has to keep his thoughts to himself!"

In November Marc was introduced to his American family in Medford, Oregon, and Sacramento, California. His grandparents, various cousins, aunts, and uncles spoiled the child with loving attention and sweets. During later visits Marc's and Grandpa Ralph's relationship grew into a wonderful friendship. Grandpa took him fishing and taught him the basics of woodsmanship. While we were in the U.S., the mind-numbing assassination of President Kennedy took place. Our time with the family on the West Coast was all too short. I left for South Africa on 2 January 1964. Dorothy and Marc followed in March, in time for his first birthday.

For the work in South Africa it was decided that we should live in Johannesburg. The pastor of the English-speaking Lutheran congregation of St. Peter by the Lake, David Nelson, and the American missionary for the North Rand, Jim Knutson, had found a strategically well-placed flat in Benoni, not far from Jan Smuts Airport to the east of Johannesburg. The flat was new. I stayed with the Knutsons until I had basic furniture and a car—a VW of course. I used the time before the family's arrival in March for a first getting-acquainted visit with the heads of the various Lutheran missions: the Swedish mission in Dundee, the Norwegian mission in Eshowe, the Hermannsburg mission with General-Superintendent Dr. von Krause, the American mission in Untunjambili with the Rev. Ted Homdrom, and a quick stop at Umpumulo Lutheran Seminary with Director Gunnar Lislerud—all in Natal—and the Berlin mission with Bishop Pakendorf in Pretoria.

This trip, the first of many, achieved what was intended: I had the opportunity to get to know the outlook of the missions and the missions of me. It didn't take a fortnight in German circles for it to be known that "Hans Florin is against apartheid!" It was the equivalent to the upper class saying, "He is not one of us!" This made my attempt at a fair and useful analysis easier: There would be some tension with the German missions, and there was a positive understanding with the others.

However, the reality of the social and intellectual structures of the country was somewhat different compared to the impressions I had from the outside—and definitely far more complex. Its complexity consisted of contrasts, the magnitude of which was greater in South Africa than elsewhere: the population of non-white (ca. twenty million) and white (ca. four million), the difference in quality of life, education, and political rights was formidable. The social tensions arising from these differences were inevitable, however, the love for country, heritage, and history—despite all the tensions—were shared by both. The demographic majority simply knew they were a part of the people to whom Africa belonged. The minority was convinced that by their economic industry, military superiority, and, therefore, political astuteness, they had the right to this incredibly beautiful and mineral-rich country.

It was quite obvious that in this complex situation people's hopes and expectations would clash at all levels of the social construct! No specific institutions—social, educational, or religious—could serve the whole population in their differing customs, habits, and experiences. After three centuries of competition and conflict there was no public law governing the structures and institutions of the South African society with equal rights and justice.

In 1948 the Afrikaans-speaking National Party formed the government, a seemingly natural constitutional law was enacted which secured the comfort and privileges of the minority ruling class at the expense of the racially different majority. This system became known as apartheid—separate development of the populations according to their traditional racial heritages. But peace and justice did not come to the South African society, neither from within nor from abroad.

This was the structure in which I was called to find the solution for a unified Lutheran witness and presence in South Africa. Three observations were foremost in forming my thinking of how to approach the topic of Lutheran service in unity:

1. The already mentioned differing missionary training was significant. In contrast to the standard training of non-German missionaries—generally the same academic course and professional status as that of the parish clergy of their respective churches—German missionaries were trained for their service abroad in specific mission seminaries. During World War II and in the following years, German missionaries from Tanganyika, Togo, and parts of Cameroon were kept in South African detention as enemy aliens. When the South African authorities started negotiations with the occupation forces for repatriation of German missionaries after 1945, the standard reply was something like this: "Please keep them where they are; we have barely enough food for those we have in our occupation zones." For whatever reason, German missionaries were kept in detention until the National Party won the election in 1948. The reflection of the new South African government seems to have been something like this: "We are prepared to release you from detention if you are willing to help us form rules and methods for developing a functioning apartheid society." Under such circumstances is it any surprise that there was grateful acceptance of this invitation? It is widely known that one fruit of German mission cooperation was the design by a son of a Berlin missionary for "Bantu education," the incidious third-rate education for blacks, which set back generations of young Africans from rising to the challenges of the new South Africa. The Lutheran missionaries, German or others, who came after World War II, did not have this experience.

2. In the first year of my stay in South Africa I had the opportunity to study minutes of meetings of the missionaries and indigenous clergy, pastors, teachers and evangelists of the different mission fields. The minutes of the Scandinavian and American missions already began to reflect a concern for a structure for their work in the future. That their mission fields should become part of a Lutheran church was obvious to them. The first such development emerged in Natal with the establishment of The Evangelical

Lutheran Church in South Africa, South Eastern Region (ELCSA-SER) with Bishop Helge Fosseus of the Svenska (Swedish) Kirkens Mission. But how should this expressly limited test structure relate to the other mission groups? The problem was with the white German-speaking Lutheran churches. They were formed for German expatriates, living in South Africa as a mixture of mission-related families; post-World War II German immigrants, often with a dubious political past; and families of German industry leaders, seeking to expand into a promising market. As explicitly Lutheran churches, they had a very lucrative contract relationship with the Evangelical Church in Germany (EKD), the umbrella organization of the Protestant dioceses in Germany.

The structurally interrelated unity of the other globally relevant churches, the Anglican and Roman Catholic communions, could not be overlooked for any future planning! While centrally structured under one head, an archbishop, the composition of their parishes reflected the population profile of their locations. Guided by their sound and solidly Gospel-oriented theology, these interracial communions were by and large critical of the apartheid ideology.

These observations and many personal discussions with people of all races and the major churches, including the apartheid-defending Dutch Reformed churches, convinced me that there should be one all-inclusive Evangelical Lutheran Church in South Africa. And this became the tenor of my concluding report, "Lutherans in South Africa." The German churches rejected the report and its author as one who did not understand the South African reality. When, at the end of our time in South Africa, we visited Cape Town, a prominent colored Lutheran pastor came to our lodgings in town, wanting to meet me and thank me for writing what non-whites could not write in their own country!

When we left South Africa later in 1965 via Victoria Falls, Nairobi, and an LWF CWM meeting in Addis Ababa, Ethiopia, I had no idea that my presence there so irritated the South African government that it was nineteen years before I would be issued another visa. It saddens me and some of the Lutheran leaders in South Africa, whom I have met since, that the all-inclusive ELCSA still does not exist. My church, the EKD, insists that if ongoing negotiations between the German churches and the infinitely larger still non-German ELCSA should decide to go together and form an all-inclusive ELCSA, the EKD would accept, recognize, and support this. It is my hope that the time will come when a united and therefore internationally credible Lutheran voice and witness can be heard from the new South Africa.

During our two years in South Africa there were dark emotional clouds over this beautiful but deeply divided and suffering land. There were also many wonderful people sharing their love and their joy over their land with us. Lasting friendships grew, friendships which were rekindled by visits back and forth between north and south. One such friendship evolved early on by meeting Bishop Pakendorf, the head of the Berlin Mission in Transvaal. Bishop Pakendorf and Dr. Brennecke, his mission director in East Berlin, did not share each others' political opinions, but respected each other's commitments to their differing tasks in the church.

One time Pakendorf invited me to come to the Berlin Mission synod meeting in the Transvaal. He was convinced that I needed to experience the respect, love, and support the mission had from the Pedi people of the northern part of this province. The place of the meeting was beyond the northern edge of Sekhukuneland, which had become an off-limits area after a serious rebellion against the authorities supporting separate development. The Transvaal road map showed only one paved road circumventing this region by a wide margin. I had heard that the Special Branch of the South African police sometimes patrolled a sand trail straight through the center and that it would be advisable to have a permit for travelling this route. I did not have such a permit, but I chanced it anyway. If one were not followed by a white Studebaker, the standard vehicle of the South

African police in those days, one would be OK. About half way through Sekhukuneland, I detected a dust cloud far behind. As fast as I dared drive, the dust cloud moved faster. Soon I could make out that it was not a white Studebaker but a long, black Packard.

In South Africa black Packards were the vehicles with which the Bantu administration outfitted local chiefs. So, why not let him pass? He must have been in a greater hurry than I needed to be. The Packard slowed and stopped behind me. A well-built and imposing man came up to me, shook my hand, and said: "I know who you are and where you are going. Please give Bishop Pakendorf my regards; he is a good man! Drive well, here you are safe." Yes, Bishop Pakendorf knew and respected this chief.

On another occasion Pakendorf organized an invitation for me to meet with a Dr. Hoffmann, a German working for the government in Pretoria. "If this man cannot convince you that the apartheid laws are really the best and only way for my land to have a safe and peaceful future . . ." —he left unsaid, "then I give up!" Of course, I was curious to meet such a man. Over dinner there was an impressive lecture on how apartheid was designed to safeguard a promising and durable black future for the indigenous peoples who simply did not have the natural gifts to guarantee their survival—or that of the white population, without which South Africa would be doomed! I had never heard such an erudite pro-apartheid lecture as this from Dr. Hoffmann.

When, after dinner, we sat with coffee and brandy by a wide picture window overlooking a vast expanse of sun-burned land with ever-changing shades of the golden-bronze of the setting sun, Dr. Hoffmann's wife, a medical doctor, told me that they did not have children and that "I would not set children into this tense South Africa!" On my way home to Benoni I thought that no more needed to be said about apartheid.

Not long after this event we read in the *Johannesburg Star* that the police reported that in the previous year more than 23,000 firearms had been stolen and not retrieved.

Bishop Pakendorf was also the first person who had told me about the existence of the Christian Institute and its remarkable director, Beyers Naude, the former Transvaal head of the Dutch Reformed Church and a member of the Afrikaans Broeder Bond, the ultimate power behind the Pretoria government. With his last sermon about "one must obey God more than man," this man resigned his position and deeply affected the South African intelligentsia.

This Christian Institute was in its time a very remarkable phenomenon which challenged many leading church leaders into re-examining their Christian witness to their nation. Its theological influence, based on sound and uncompromising biblical interpretation, did not condone any support from Holy Scripture for separate development on racial grounds!

The 1973 publication of a comprehensive and critically constructive report of the political commission of the Study Project of Christianity in Apartheid Society (Spro-cas) *South Africa's Political Alternatives*, edited by Peter Randall and sponsored by the South African Council of Churches (SACC) and Christian Institute of Southern Africa (CISA) contains the thought and spirit of many critical persons of professional prominence who shared Beyers Naude's deeply worried concern for a stable future for all who live in and contribute to South Africa. This report represents the studies of the Spro-cas group between 1969 and 1973. Without the prophetic witness of Beyers Naude, who at times led both the SACC and the CISA, the prospects for a peaceful future for that country would have been very bleak indeed!

Needless to say, the Christian Institute was not at all in sync with the official apartheid policy. Government strove to stop, both legally and later also illegally, the free and unopposed functioning of CISA, both within South Africa and abroad. Help came to CISA from the ecumenical movement in Geneva and from the EKD Office of Protestant Mission Assistance (EAGWM) in Hamburg, with which I was later associated. The small Reformed Church of

Northwest Germany secured Beyers Naude's pension, which he had forfeited when he resigned his former position in the Dutch Reformed Church. For many who knew and worked with Beyers Naude, this man had become the shining example of Christian discipleship!

Later, during my time with the EKD Mission Assistance Office, Beyers was a regular guest whenever his travels took him to Germany. Because this man was an effective thorn in the flesh of the South African government, its consul general in Hamburg considered it his duty to be informed whenever Beyers was in town. This poor consul never received his information and thereby missed out on "hosting" this brave man. Through those contacts I somehow inherited the consul's displeasure which resulted in my identification as "South Africa's worst enemy in Germany."

Another churchman critical of apartheid South Africa was the Roman Catholic Bishop Dennis Hurley of Durban. In the early 1960s I met Bishop Hurley a couple of times and began to realize that a bishop in the globe-encompassing Roman Catholic Church had quite naturally been aware that his was the *one* church in which Christians of all races found their spiritual home with dignity. With this attitude he became an uncomfortable citizen for his government, which must have persuaded the Vatican to look for another candidate than Hurley for the position of Archbishop of the Roman Catholic Province of Southern Africa. In 1984, after obtaining my first South African visa in nineteen years, I met him once more.

For the first day of my first return to South Africa since 1965, the South African Council of Churches had booked me on a flight to Durban to see Bishop Denis Hurley. Before take-off, with doors still open, a man came to the door for a quick exchange. The stewardess came to my seat, picked up my boarding pass in the empty seat next to me, returned to the door and nodded an affirmation. This procedure, I was convinced, would result in being tailed by the Special Branch of the South African police after arrival in Durban.

The colleague from Diaconia, an inter-church aid service for needs in the tight location around Durban's Indian Curry Market as well as in townships, realized immediately that evasive actions were needed to lose the tail. We changed cars twice and ended up unmolested at the bishop's residence.

This was a wonderful reunion with a man who saw so clearly the desperate situation of South Africa. He loved his country but more so he loved and cared for his diocese. Because by then I was general secretary of the World Association for Christian Communication (WACC), I suggested making a video portrait of this exceptional man. Unfortunately, this suggestion drowned in my action-packed WACC work schedule.

Years later, in January 2004, I was once more in South Africa. I wanted to be in touch with Bishop Hurley, to apologize for not following up my proposal. From Pietermaritzburg we had a very fine twenty-minute telephone conversation. He dismissed my *mea culpa* confession right away: "Don't we all have such sins of omission—and too many of them?" Most of all, however, I wanted to share with him my ecumenical insight that at some time we all would have to return to Mother Church. His reply: "Oh, please don't hurry. There is much in my church that has to be changed first before we can become truly *one!*"

The next morning at breakfast I heard on the radio that Bishop Hurley had died that morning during mass in church. What a loss! And there could not be any sensible or prophetic response to this death. Our talk that afternoon could likely have been the last before he was called to his Master's rest.

There is one other focal point throughout our stay in South Africa and well beyond—the Rev. Ted Homdrom and his family. In the good tradition of "a missionary can tackle anything," this man covered many positions in the emerging structure of ELCSA, including the first tentative coordinator of the operational budgets of the cooperating missions, a position which later consolidated into the ELCSA general secretary and treasurer. Ultimately this task was located in Johannesburg, in Khotso House, which housed the offices of the SACC, the office of the first African presiding bishop of ELCSA, Dr. Manas Buthelezi, and eventually also remnants of the Christian Institute. No wonder then that this house was bombed in 1988.

The context of knowing each other on a more personal basis had nothing to do with my analysis of the Lutheran presence in South Africa. It was in mid-1964, during the South African winter, that Ted Homdrom had heard that British Overseas Airways Corporation (BOAC) had a new passenger jet for the South Africa route: the VC-10. This interested Ted, a World War II navigator of the US Eighth Air force, who had flown thirty B17 missions over Germany out of East Anglia, England.

The first VC-10 arrival—the date is lost in memory— was scheduled for about 6:30 a.m. into Jan Smuts Airport. We left Benoni in time. I knew exactly where we would have the best location for observing an approach within seconds of touch down. The time, 6:30, came—but no VC-10. I became fascinated with Ted's missions over Germany and their timing. A few were along what surviving navigators called "Flack Alley," south of Wesel via Dinslaken to Oberhausen on the western edge of the heavily industrialized Ruhr area. And is it not a coincidence of place and time that the 88-battery in which I was serving as a fifteen-year-old *Luftwaffenhelfer* would have been involved in the radar direction of our guns? Many times during later meetings in South Africa we came back to this coincidence, which had grown into a friendship.

However, another coincidence of much later was not yet on the horizon. Mission kids (MKs) did not only grow up on mission stations in the rural hinterland. They were boarding school students, living in the mission hostel at Eshowe, the capital of Zululand. For me it was only much later that I became aware of Ted and Betty's three children: two boys, split by daughter Ev.

Hamburg

Before we left for South Africa there was talk in Germany that mission should be closer to the church. In fact, I had heard this from my Guetersloh Superintendent Heinrich Lohmann. As he also was the head of the Rhenish Mission, he was ideally suited to be involved in developing this idea. At that time he had no firm commitment to becoming personally involved, but I was convinced that if such an opportunity should come about, I would very much like to be part of it. Yes, such an office of church concern for world mission should be anchored in the EKD (Evangelical Church in Germany), the umbrella for all Protestant churches in Germany. And no, this office should not be at the German Mission Council in Hamburg.

From the one or two letters we exchanged while in South Africa, I learned that the Protestant Cooperative for World Mission (*Evangelische Arbeitsgemeinschaft fuer Welt Mission*—EAGWM) would be an EKD-office, but would be in Hamburg. And yes, if after South Africa I would like to join him in Hamburg, he would secure a position for me.

In my mind I saw the Hamburg job as somewhat of a continuation of my job in South Africa, linking mission and church closer together. In South Africa it was the various missions and their mission fields which were the established entities. In Germany it would be the EKD and her member churches which represented the established constant; the many mission societies would be the flexible element which I thought should be linked to, if not integrated into, the church. This, in short, was my concept—a concept which proved to be less flexible than I would have wished.

But what was the make-up of the church and mission in early 1966? By 1966 the EKD and her member churches had become well recognized. In addition they had grown into comfortably endowed institutions. The pre-1945 tensions between *Deutsche Christen* and Confessing Churches had, in my mind, been too easily put aside by absorbing the perhaps patriotically misguided Nazi Christians into a church which, right after World War II, personified one of the very few stable institutions in German society. After the war this church had confessed publicly her failings for not condemning more forcefully the massive destruction which Hitler's morally defunct Germany had inflicted on Europe and beyond. She should have had more time for healing and reconciliation within herself, but rather rushed the administrative incorporation of those who preferred to ignore this confession. Nevertheless, this church had become recognized internationally because through currency reform and constitutionally embedded church tax it had become comfortably wealthy. The EKD and her member churches had become respected members of the ecumenical movement. At that stage their international contacts extended primarily to similarly established ecumenical sister churches in North America and Europe, including Scandinavia and Switzerland. These contacts helped the German churches broaden their awareness beyond Europe to what was then called the mission fields and younger churches in Africa and Asia.

In those years Germany became conscious of the political tool of foreign aid—a tool which Konrad Adenauer had considered useful for foreign policy, especially in the developing world. Foreign aid for pre-World War I German colonies existed; could there also be aid for still existing German mission fields? Individual German mission societies had already begun to benefit from this thinking. But they felt German foreign aid should not be restricted to former German historical connections. So the Protestant Cooperative for World Mission (PCWM) was furnished with a minor aid package for the support of wider ecumenical initiatives in the area of world mission. At its beginning the PCWM's List of Needs comprised projects amounting to about 1.6 million *Deutsche Marks* per year. A decade later this list had grown to 16 million *Deutsche Marks*.

In PCWM it was my concern that what little funds were at our disposal should not be dispensed to projects over which we, or German mission societies, had control. Rather it should be PCWM's trademark that it respected the overseas partners' dignity and capability to conceive and administer their projects responsibly according to their own terms. Perhaps it was in response to this attitude that PCWM's aid budget never came anywhere near to those of Diaconia or general aid institutions as Bread for the World or the Protestant Development Service. In the 1960s and 1970s it was so much easier to raise funds for projects over which those who provided the funds influenced a certain and approved measure of control.

To link or integrate some forty different mission societies into the churches was quite another matter. Had there been, like in the Scandinavian or American sister churches, fully integrated mission departments, staffed to standards of their clergy personnel, there would have been no need for further integration. But, as such an idea was completely unknown in Germany, there were problems. Neither missions nor churches were at first over-enthusiastic. Part of the lack of enthusiasm might well have to do with post-World War II ambiguity of the term "evangelical." Is it a conservative awakening type of piety or is it simply "Protestant" as the generic term for Lutheran, Reformed, or United, as in the old Prussian Union?

However, little by little arrangements were hammered out by which both former missions and future international church outlook would benefit. What emerged were seven regional mission centers with administrative control under one or more territorial churches, staffed by a younger set of professionals with open minds and eyes for what was going on in the world—and why! I am not surprised that the relationship of such regional mission centers with their own churches abroad has borne much fruit in terms of stability. The head of one such regional center, the Vereinigte Evangelische Mission (VEM), is now a pastor of the Lutheran Church of Tanzania, the Rev. Dr. Fidon Mwombeki. Without PCWM such developments would not have come about. The consequent conclusion of this development is the merger of the German Mission Council and PCWM into the Evangelical Mission Work in Germany. The staff maintains relations with World Council of Churches (WCC) and Lutheran World Federation (LWF) mission departments, looks after the Mission Academy in Hamburg, and publishes a wide range of books and brochures of interest for a mission-oriented public. These publications cover country-specific reviews from Africa and Asia, report from ecumenical assemblies, and contribute to the ongoing debate about the theology of mission.

So much for the context in which the PCWM began and, after a decade, ceased to exist as a separate administrative unit. In this decade the PCWM had seen the completion of the integration of mission and church into the seven regional mission centers. Its ecumenical assistance program, known as the PCWM List of Needs, was consolidated with the wider Protestant Development Service.

For its public outreach, the PCWM had been given the Rogation Sunday on the Fifth Sunday after Easter for illustrating to the Protestant public the rapidly changing reality of world mission around the world. Some of this activity is now carried on by the Protestant Mission Work in Germany. But many of the activities of PCWM's dedicated staff merit further attention.

When I joined the PCWM, Heinrich Lohmann employed one journalist, Mr. Heinz Melzer, for informing the Protestant Press Service (EPD) in Frankfurt about PCWM's existence and its intended purpose. In the early days Lohmann and I visited the local churches to invite them to provide an annual contribution for our List of

Needs. It was important that in each diocesan budget there should be a position to support international and ecumenical projects. It was not always easy to convince the churches of new and growing challenges in world mission beyond support for their favored mission societies and traditional mission fields. We crisscrossed the country by rail and flew to Berlin for the statutory meetings of the EKD agencies—especially the EKD Foreign Office in Frankfurt and the Diaconia, strong points in Stuttgart and Düsseldorf. I had my problems with the EKD Foreign Office ever since I had seen its head travel with diplomatic pomp and dispense generous support to the German-speaking churches in South Africa, whose members on the average earned at least ten times as much as their brothers and sisters in ELCSA. This troubled me in South Africa and annoyed me—prompting me to enquire in Germany whether this colleague might not be of better service in an internationally less exposed position. This remained wishful thinking. Some church leaders, who agreed with my concern, admitted that, unfortunately, the man could not be removed from his position. In the 1960s these insensitivities vis-à-vis racial injustices were not uncommon in German church circles. But it was in such an atmosphere that PCWM had to impart the rapidly changing reality of world mission. Much of PCWM's information outreach was directed at these "innocent" prejudices.

Another, more personal, incident from the early fundraising history happened in Leer, East Friesia. On arrival at the diocesan office of the small North West Reformed Church, my name raised interest: "Are you related to Pastor Florin in Freren?"

"Do you mean my Uncle Fritz in Freren?"

"The very same—and you dare ask us for money? Your uncle is 102, and we still pay his pension." This all ended in a friendly smile. North West Reformed became a steady supporter.

It wasn't all that long before it was obvious that the PCWM needed more staff. Our first journalist, Mr Melzer, fell ill. Before his death he recommended that a colleague from the *Sueddeutsche Zeitung*, Klaus Viehweger, might replace him. This proved to be an excellent choice: crystal-clear writing, wide ranging connections among his colleagues, fresh thinking, and new ideas. For Rogation Sunday he developed a challenging poster series. This and additional information of the new and less prejudicial mission thinking reached some 13,000 parishes each spring. Soon also Wolfgang Erk followed as the new editor for an almost defunct mission quarterly, which he changed to a color monthly with gratifying success. Wolfgang later became the publisher of the renowned Radius Publishing House in Stuttgart. We were fortunate to add a young pastoral intern whose theologically sound reflections influenced all of PCWM's publications. This man, Hartwig Liebich, became, after my leaving Hamburg, a vital contact to Beyers Naude and the Christian Institute. For this purpose he was placed in Harare, Zimbabwe, from where one could travel with low profile as a tourist to Johannesburg. After the merger, Hartwig returned to his church, the North Elbian Lutheran Church, to continue his ministry as pastor and later as *Probst* of Volksdorf, one of the largest regional circuits in his church.

The PCWM information department soon garnered respect for quality. The most ambitious feature from this department merits a closer look: the Rogation poster campaign with thoughtful pictorials of everyday life in our sister churches abroad—schooling, healing, enlightened parenting, and helping to prevent illnesses of poverty rather than of affluence.

One poster featured the new Peters-projection of planet earth, with its much criticized distortions but accurate presentation of the different national extensions in relation to each other. Along the margin was a quotation from Psalm 89:13: "The north and the south, thou hast created them"—thus indicating that our Creator God knew full well how he wanted the poles of north and south to relate to each other, rather than our traditional Mercator projection which bestows with imperious abandon on the northern hemisphere a land mass quite out of proportion to its actual size. We published this projection with 100,000 copies. Church World Service (CWS) in New York took this up with another 100,000. Later, Dr. Arno Peters, the universal historian and originator, thanked Klaus Viehweger with a comment something like this: "Without you, without the PCWM, my projection would not have had the wider breakthrough beyond the level in which it was almost drowned by universal criticism." Years later, after my retirement, Peters and his partner came to Sidlesham for a memorable lunch.

Another poster was met with similar but this time primarily church criticism. There was a healthy baby in the arms of a model torso with a superbly formed healthy bosom. Its message: "He needs mother's milk, not milk powder!" It was our mistake that this bosom obviously had never suckled a baby. On the Saturday before publication I received a call from a pretty high-placed church leader and lawyer: "Stop this publication; it is profane!" I rejected this order—for the sake of the many ill-nourished children I had seen in Africa. Although this rejection was perhaps a poor career move, now in old age I am sure I was morally right.

The third poster, in my mind our most ingenious one, had Michaelangelo's *Last Supper* in every detail—except that all heads, other than the head of Christ, belonged to affluent Europeans with differing expressions of self-satisfaction. This poster was disliked by many for being naughty and blasphemous. But we also had heard that this poster had made many people think of some tension between their styles of living and their faith.

One last feature of the information department was the journalist trips to what in some circles were thought to be controversial projects. Through Viehweger's acquaintance with many of the best journalists in the land, we had two or three such ventures: to Egypt and the Holy Land for meeting Muslims and Christians as neighbors, and Rome, from where the powerful global information of the Vatican via press and radio emanates. I accompanied him only on the trip to Rome. On the agenda was a visit to Radio Vaticana, to a Roman Catholic missions operation with an outlook similar to that of PCWM, which we had sometimes supported, and to the United Nations Food and Agriculture Administration (UNFAO). Our occasional help to the Roman Catholic mission office irritated a journalist of a Catholic paper in Aachen. His report of the trip had a critical note. The other journalists advised not to correct the one-sided view published in Aachen, where the German Roman Catholic office of MISSIO is located, with which PCWM had the most open and collegial relationship—they would sort out the matter—and they did! And nothing more was heard of that.

Klaus Viehweger died in the early stages of merger. My successor, Dr. Martin Lehmann-Habeck from the head office of the Berlin church, asked me if I could do a thanksgiving service for Klaus: "You have known him longer than I have!" I had been at a thanksgiving service at Union Theological Seminary in New York for Dr. Lehmann, its gifted sacred music master. Viehweger's secretary selected and read some passages from Klaus' ever so thoughtful and well-written book, *Weltmissions-Konferenz Bangkok: Samudhprakarn, Kilometer 31*, which reflected on what the EKD churches could have done for their sister churches in the poorer world abroad. After each passage the assembled staff responded "and his church has heard him not!" We closed this service by sharing bread and wine silently with each other.

There was a parallel event to the PCWM support policy, "no aid to projects other than in the third world." This policy was shared by Church World Service, the interchurch aid department of the National Council of Churches of the USA (NCC USA). This agency had asked me whether I could make available some funds for a small medical clinic and upgraded ambulance in Mound Bayou, the first all-black, incorporated town in Mississippi after the U.S. Civil War. Interracial prejudice in New York could not justify their (Church World Service) allocating funds to a little black town in the U.S.A. A contribution from Germany could expose such prejudice. With this request from this reputable organization I was able to persuade our distribution committee to assign some 120,000 *Deutsche Marks* for this project.

In New York a great thing was made of this. At NCC's expense, air travel was arranged to the Mississippi capital, Jackson, and from there a small one-engine, one-hour flight to Mound Bayou. I was accompanied on this trip by the son of the editor-owner of the only liberal newspaper in the state of Mississippi in the 1960s. The mayor of Mound Bayou told of the socially disruptive consequences of an anti-black sentiment still very much alive in the South of the 1960s. It was there in a small restaurant below the Mississippi River dyke that I had my first and only catfish dinner. Before departing the next morning I met with Mound Bayou's police chief. His stories matched those of the mayor. One in particular I shall not forget: Not far from Mound Bayou is the north-south freeway to Memphis, Tennessee, the closest major hospital town. It happened more than once that after a car crash that some wounded lay on the freeway. When the Mound Bayou ambulance was the first to arrive, the police chief said the response was, "No, thank you, we won't take a nigger ambulance. We will wait for the white ambulance from Memphis." The chief of police's story ended with this stark comment: "It has been known that some people injured on the freeway would rather die than be carried by a black ambulance to Memphis." When we parted he thanked me for what I had done for Mound Bayou, and he undid the Mound Bayou police badge from his tunic to take home with me in memory of this black town in the south of the U.S.A. It now has pride of place on my desk in Chimes Cottage in Sidlesham, West Sussex, United Kingdom.

Through the journalist trips PCWM had a good standing in these circles. The head of the Protestant Press Service (EPD) in Frankfurt, a former colleague from LWF days in Geneva, approached me once as to whether I could please arrange a religious retreat for journalists. I am ashamed to admit that my reaction was not all that different from that of my inter-church aid colleagues in New York. Why should I waste my time, energy and funds for such a group—known, with a certain amount of prejudice, for rarely darkening the threshold of a church door? Besides, the funds entrusted to PCWM were to go to needs abroad—in the third world. Now that I write this I am aware that this reaction was wrong—totally wrong! It has become one of my primary sins of omission. A Lutheran pastor could well have brought some pastoral care to these professionals, many of whom I have come to treasure as solid and honest human beings.

Last but definitely not least of PCWM achievements was the Theological Teachers Exchange Program (TTEP). At the time, during which former mission fields merged and graduated into independent churches under indigenous leadership, the need for substantial pastoral training became obvious. Schools of theology were envisioned, ideally in the form of theological faculties of established universities abroad or as a strong ecumenical signal standing alone, open for students from diaspora churches in a Muslim-dominated world.

As requests came from Makerere, the leading university of the British Empire in East Africa, Dumaguete City University on Cebu in the Philippines, and the Near East School of Theology (NEST) in Beirut, Lebanon, the PCWM board, which included a couple of theology professors, decided that these requests should become part of the List of Needs. Prof. Hans-Werner Gensichen, missiologist of Heidelberg University and New Testament Professor Eduard Lohse of Hamburg University became the core of the TTEP committee.

This program raised some interest among young Ph.D. qualified candidates for an academic career in theology. Great sensitivity was required for selecting persons for usually delicate postings abroad. I remember one rather self-conscious young man who expected a posting at a coastal capital with a safe beach for his daughters and an airport with direct flights to Germany for himself. Beirut would have suited him fine, but he was not suited for Beirut.

For the necessary administrative continuity, PCWM needed an experienced and capable staff. Ute Pelkmann, former secretary at the LWF Department of Theology, was available and willing to join us in Hamburg. Ute's appointment brought the added benefit of securing the fantastic and detailed archival brain, and the competent as well as speedy text composition, of Ute's husband Frank Kuerschner to PCWM's Information department.

During my time with PCWM I had the privilege of visiting four young theological teachers at their assignments: two in Dumaguete City, the Philippines; one at Makerere University in Uganda; and one at NEST in Beirut. After a WCC Commission for World Mission and Evangelism (CWME) meeting in Japan I could tag on my visit to Dumaguete City. The theology department of Dumaguete University was, indeed, grateful for the added depth of courses which our teachers had brought there.

The university campus bordered the magnificently blue Pacific Ocean. From the beach it was only a short swim to a coral reef, the likes of which I had before only seen in pictures. On one afternoon the swimming excursion to the reef took longer than planned. When the 4:30 p.m. Philippine Air arrival was low above us on its final approach to Dumaguete Airport, Dorothea, the young wife of one of our professors, warned me to hurry back to the beach before the short tropical dusk would blur our vision. Rather than the forty-minute swim along the reef to the beach, she suggested a straight twenty-minute turn directly from reef to beach: "Please swim as flatly as you can; there are colorless spikes on the way which may slit your belly." I didn't need any further encouragement to make it to the beach as fast as I could. On all fours I crossed the beach to rest by a palm tree. My lungs pumped heavily, even with some pain. Why was Dorothea not yet back? Then I saw her white swimming cap crisscrossing along the way and diving at times. This wonderful young lady rose out of the shallow waters and came effortlessly, without any hard breathing with a smile on her face, across the beach to the palm tree. She handed me some sea stars and unusual shells—in memory of the Dumaguete Coral Reef. At that moment I had confirmation that my youth was over; I had become an old man! Unfortunately the beautiful sea stars and shells did not survive the trip home via Hong Kong and another meeting.

My trips to Makerere in Kampala, Uganda, and NEST in Beirut had different, not foreseeable political surprises. The visit with my friend Dr. Wilhelm Wille, our man in Makerere, was part of a multi-purpose trip to East Africa, mostly Nairobi. For some years there had been strategically interesting projects on our List of Needs in the area of communication: the publishing house of the Anglican Church in Kenya and the radio studio of the All Africa Conference of Churches (AACC) producing programs for transmission by Radio Voice of the Gospel—both in Nairobi. These projects were sponsored and advised by the World Association for Christian Communication (WACC). As WACC and PCWM had already enjoyed a preferential ecumenical cooperation for some time, I had become a member of WACC's Executive Committee. On this trip I was accompanied by Dr Robert Geisendoerfer, from Munich, Germany, the treasurer of WACC. He wanted to acquaint himself with both PCWM supported projects in Nairobi.

On the Lufthansa flight from Munich to Nairobi via Kampala I ended up in an aisle seat next to an African-American woman, a TWA fare coordinator. This was her first trip to what she considered her rightful home. During the approach to Kampala, Africa's uniquely red soil came closer and closer. In her excitement she challenged me concerning what claim I, as "a whitey," might have to this land. My explanation did not wash with her. I was glad I could get off in Kampala. Dr. Geisendoerfer would continue to Nairobi. We would meet there in three days at the New Stanley Hotel.

Dr. Wille's placement raised an ecclesiastic question. In the university chapel he had, as a Lutheran pastor, regular Sunday afternoon services for the numerous Lutheran students from Tanzania. Would it be possible to have a Lutheran communion service once a month on a Sunday morning as an ecumenical alternative to the Anglican sung eucharist? No, this was not possible in the Anglican province of East Africa! But his teaching contributions to the theological faculty were highly appreciated. Among Dr. Wille's colleagues were some African lecturers who later became known as originators and leaders of an indigenous African theology. Among them was Dr. John Mbiti of Makerere, who would become especially noteworthy.

A day later Dr. Wille (known among friends as Willi) took me through Kampala. On Telegraph Hill—a name from British colonial days—Willi explained the layout of the capital of Uganda. Although there could be some unrest off and on, nothing major could possibly happen now because Uganda's first president after independence, Apolo Milton Obote, had left for the Commonwealth Conference in Singapore. "He would never have left if there had been any chance of trouble!" As the Anglican bishop could not tolerate a Lutheran eucharist on a Sunday morning, there was no need to stay another day. I could get the first DC-3 flight to Nairobi one day earlier than booked.

The next morning over breakfast in Nairobi we heard of Idi Amin's coup. A tank blocking the departure hall had fired one round into the group checking in for the flight that should have been mine. There had been several fatalities.

I immediately went to the German embassy. Willi had recommended I should get to know the new ambassador, a young, bright SPD diplomat, who had a real heart for and understanding of Africa. I told this man about Dr. Wille— "Oh, yes, a good man, just right for Makerere"—and asked him whether he would keep an eye on him and his family.

The ambassador called the Lufthansa office in downtown Kampala, which confirmed the coup. "We all hide under our desks. There is a lot of machine gun noise outside in the street!" And, indeed, there was; we could hear it clearly.

Later I called Dr. Wille's home number and got through immediately. We talked about work and family, but each time I asked about the coup, the line went dead. This happened from the All Africa Council of Churches (AACC) general secretary's house, too. Canon Burgess Carr was worried he could be targeted if there were more calls from his house. So I had the last and longest call with Willi from a call box in the Nairobi Hilton. And luck would have it that on my way out of the hotel I recognized the African-American TWA lady on the other side of the street—on the arm of a young, short-trousered British colonial gentleman.

After his term to Makerere, Dr. Wille became my trusted colleague and friend at PCWM in Hamburg. His integrity and straight talking was not appreciated everywhere—least of all in the EKD Synod. In one annual report to synod he prescribed the "redistribution of wealth" as much needed medicine for healing the social and economic injustices in today's world. Without back-up by his chairman and in connection with the on-going merger, Dr. Wille requested a transfer to a parish and was offered the rural parish of Borsfleet, behind the dikes of the Elbe River. His ministry for ten years in the notoriously spiritually dry soil of his village was in the end understood by some parishioners, mostly by those who were weekenders from Hamburg.

Similar in outlook and ecumenical experience was PCWM's theological teacher placement in the Near East School of Theology (NEST) in Beirut—an ecumenically oriented inter-church institution associated with Beirut University. Dr. Paul Loeffler had worked in world mission offices in London and Geneva. At NEST he came in contact with orthodox students of the Syriac, Coptic, and Armenian churches. NEST became a preferred training ground for promising students from the member churches of the Near East Council of Churches (NECC). One of Paul Loeffler's students later became the Catholicos of the Western Armenian Church in Antelias.

PCWM not only procured theological teachers for NEST, but was also instrumental in completing the costly construction of the NEST facility. Its grounds were limited, so it was decided to build underground. The deep and solid rock base allowed planning for two underground levels. One became a major oratory and concert hall; the other provided classrooms, a library, and the radio studio for programs which the NECC broadcast via Radio Voice of the Gospel in Ethiopia. Both NEST and the NECC studio were major projects of PCWM—and both of these were, in light of the political unrest in the region, considered bomb proof.

On one of my visits to Beirut in the early phases of the civil war in Lebanon, I stayed with Paul and Ingrid Loeffler. They had a spacious penthouse in downtown Beirut. The view from there was breathtaking. On that occasion the view was not the main attraction. Owing to political unrest, there was a curfew in place between 10:00 p.m. and 7:00 a.m. For Beirut this was an unheard-of restriction. Real life only just began there at 10:00 p.m. and lasted rather noisily at least until 3:00 a.m. The uniqueness of this curfew was that it affected only Lebanese. Foreigners could walk freely about, with passport of course, for inspections at liberally placed check points. The fact that it was a full moon might have increased the temptation to test the curfew. It worked! This became the only quiet and unhurried night I ever had in Beirut. We walked in the direction of the famous Corniche, the shore route along Beirut's beach on the Mediterranean. We shared memories of our different ecumenical staff and conference experiences and remained untempted by restaurants or wine bars. They were closed; this was a curfew after all.

Through the ecumenical orientation of the projects which PCWM supported, it was no surprise that I should be called to serve on international committees. In followup to the 1968 WCC Assembly in Uppsala, I was asked to chair the WCC DICARWS (Department of Inter-Church Aid,

Refugees, and World Service) project subcommittee for three years. Its staff coordinator was Jan Fischer, a Swiss national. His preparation of project applications for DICARWS support was similar to the format we had developed in the LWF. Most of the requests were accepted unanimously. Occasionally a German committee member, Klaus Poser, head of the EKD Development Service in Bonn, asked for more details. I took this as intent to tease me—his colleague from Hamburg in competition for EKD funds—rather than doubting the preparation of project applications. Klaus Poser later became the director of DICARWS.

However, while I was chairman of the project subcommittee, the president of the church in Westphalia had been called to be chairman of the DICARWS committee, governing all activities of that department. There could be moments, especially in policy debates about priorities in ecumenical aid, when we did not see eye-to-eye. It was only years later after a lecture I presented to the Westphalian circuit of the Knights of St. John, that we had a friendly and collegial exchange of our common ecumenical past.

Shortly after assuming the role as the project subcommittee chairman, the invitation to take over the position for the European Regional Executive Committee (EUREC) of the United Bible Societies (UBS) came. Through Heinrich Lohmann's assessment of the limited support from the small and very local Bible societies in Germany, it was decided that the global work of the UBS should have a more substantial contribution through PCWM's List-of-Needs. This support became known as the Lohmann million.

It was the idea of the outgoing EUREC chairman, the Dutch Baron van Tuyll van Serooskerken, that thanks to PCWM's generosity, a German might become his successor. When I was in hospital for a leg operation, my secretary called me: "There is a Baron Tuyll in the office to see you, and your being in hospital won't stop him." He was in fact on his way to the hospital. Yes, I had heard of this UBS giant and his heroic and sovereign treatment of a German officer who had come to arrest him in May 1941. In fluent German he made short shrift of this poor lieutenant: "I will only speak with your commanding general!" I knew that a man that stubborn could not be stopped from coming to my hospital bed. However, the matron was even more clever: She rearranged her office for the imminent meeting with the Dutch baron, with tea and Scottish shortbread ready. This started my chairmanship of EUREC. EUREC's meetings were prepared by a regional staff in Bassersdorf, near Zurich. My first regional secretary was the Rev. Svere Smaadahl of Norway.

During our annual regional meetings I let myself first be guided by a sympathy for the poorer societies and offices, such as Rome and Belgrade, vis-à-vis the domineering force of strong supporting societies in Europe, such as the Netherlands, Norway, Scotland, and Britain. It was only years later, after I had become UBS regional secretary, that I realized that Renzo Bertalot was more a thorn in the flesh than the eloquent defender of the poor and dependent Bible offices.

As EUREC chairman I became aware of how limited the support for UBS was from the numerous little Bible societies in Germany. Uli Fick, a former colleague in the LWF, with Radio Voice of the Gospel, and now president of the Privilegierte Wuertembergische Bibelanstalt in Stuttgart, invited me to address this motley crowd at their annual meeting in Ratzeburg. My only idea for this diversified group was that there should be only *one* German Bible society. On a walk after lunch along Lake Ratzeburg, Uli made clear to me that I had offended practically my whole audience—and added with a grin: "But, of course you are right. None of the worthy and tradition-rich local Bible societies have either the necessary leadership strength nor the well-to-do hinterland to be a convincing voice for Germany in the wider UBS world." Not long after the post-lunch walk came a query from the Wuertembergische Anstalt—by the way the by far biggest Bible society in the land—whether I would know of a person who could become the over-all director of the Bible conglomerate in Stuttgart, which included Biblia Druck, a renowned thin-paper printing press.

Not long after this enquiry I came across the Rev. Dr. Siegfried Meurer, a ranking staff member in the Diaconia department of the powerful Protestant Church of the Rhineland, with headquarters in Düsseldorf. I liked Dr. Meurer because he had become critical of the diaconal policy under which he had to work. Might he be interested in a change? Could it be as far afield as Stuttgart and the world of Bible mission and distribution? "Well, I don't know this world—but one could try!" The leadership qualities and sound theological outlook resulted in his call to Stuttgart. At first not everybody in Stuttgart, Uli Fick included, found it easy to get along with the new director, Dr. Meurer. But in a few years this man had so changed the German Bible scene that it became possible for one strong and central German Bible society to emerge in Stuttgart, the support of which increased the UBS world budget rapidly to the point of becoming second only to the mighty American Bible Society (ABS).

My EUREC chairmanship went with me to the World Association for Christian Communication in London for a few years.

London

World Association for Christian Communication
1976-1986

In early 1976 the World Association for Christian Communication (WACC) was in an unstable situation. The merger of the Christian Literature Fund (CLF) with the World Association for Christian Broadcasting (WACB) had barely been completed. The merged agency had agreed to be known as the World Association for Christian Communication, but there were undercurrents of competitive mistrust in both the CLF and WACB staff and committees. The origins of both organizations historically and geographically were too dissimilar for a smooth integration.

The CLF had its origins in the nineteenth-century mission fields of the major non-Roman Catholic churches. After the groundbreaking World Mission Conference of 1911 in Edinburgh, participating churches had begun to accept that its witness and service to Jesus Christ's ministry and mission merited greater cooperation. The 1911 Edinburgh event led to the installation of the World Council of Churches (WCC) in 1948. Soon after its beginning, the WCC integrated the offices of the International Mission Council from London into its Geneva campus as the WCC Commission for World Mission and Evangelism (WCC CWME). Thus the CLF and its independent funding structure had become a part of the WCC CWME, through which such tasks as interdenominational and ecumenical printing and publishing for the newly emerging churches in Asia and

Africa could be supported. In its funding structure and policy, CWME differed explicitly from the support policy of the WCC Department of Inter-Church Aid, Refugees, and World Service (WCC DICARWS)—thus safeguarding the editorial independence of the new indigenous churches. With its staff and committee tradition, the CLF brought a dowry of about 1.5 million dollars to WACC.

At the time of the CLF WACB merger, Dr. Philip Potter was the director of the WCC Commission for World Mission and Evangelism in Geneva. During a good number of years in Hamburg I had been a member of Philip's commission. Through many meetings, our understanding of the challenge of the world mission of the church had reached a comfortable affinity. Our friendship grew with the fortification Philip served up in the form of respectable West Indian rum punches. His vision and ministry merit some comments.

Philip was born in Dominica—one of the islands of the British West Indies. Prior to coming to Geneva he had been the head of the Methodist Mission Board in London. Together with many of his colleagues I was very pleased when in 1972 Philip Potter became the first non-European general secretary of the WCC.

It was during Philip Potter's watch that the WCC challenged all its member churches to support The Ecumenical Program to Combat Racism. Its purpose was to assist organizations in opposing political and economic oppression fueled by racist attitudes, such as the South African apartheid regime and similar situations, some of which were in the Near East. The resolution to set up this program was supported by a majority of member churches of what was then called the third world. A number of Western churches, which funded the ecumenical movement, met this program with critical aversion. The Evangelical Church in Germany (EKD) member churches shared this critical response and declared that church tax revenue could not be diverted to this program. Any German support came from personal collections. Churches in the West shied away from what were seen to be lawless terror organizations. This attitude of aversion was spreading widely and contributed to the decline of funding for a movement which from its beginnings had upheld the ecumenical ideal.

My friend Philip's name remained associated with this program to combat racism well into his years of retirement. In Germany Philip's friends once met him and confirmed that the program was right for its time and necessary to unmask the destructive force of unreflected racism. Years after this I visited Philip once more in Luebeck, Germany, where we remembered the days of unresolved criticism and still lingering lack of understanding of what the churches' role of being disciples of our Lord should be.

The origins of the WACB go back to the late 1940s. After World War II Bishop George Bell invited European Christian religious broadcasters to Chichester, his diocese, so that their messages could contribute to the healing of a lingering enmity among the people in Europe. With the liberation of Europe from the morally corrupt Nazi occupation, churches throughout that continent had found a new freedom to bring Christ's message to the people. Most national broadcasting networks had religious services conceived and produced by Christians. It was with these people that Bishop Bell wanted to form an association of professional religious broadcasters. The World Association of Christian Broadcasters became the third ecumenical organization—after the World Council of Churches and the United Bible Societies—that Bishop Bell, the ecumenical giant of Chichester, had been instrumental in bringing to life.

The core members of the WACB were the religious departments of the British Broadcasting Corporation; the Nederlandse Christelijke Radio Vereniging (Dutch Christian Radio Association), a Dutch interdenominational Christian network; and the national broadcasting networks of Scandinavia and Switzerland, including the religious portfolios of Radio Deutschland, German radio, and the German regional services: West Deutscher Rundfunk (West German

Radio), Nord Deutscher Rundfunk (North German Radio), Sued Deutscher Rundfunk (South German Radio), and Bayern (Bavaria). Soon also the religious broadcasting units of the National Council of Churches–USA joined the WACB. These units transmitted their programs through differing contracts with the national, mostly commercial, networks ABC (American Broadcasting Corporation), CBS (Central Broadcasting System), NBC (National Broadcasting Corporation), and PBS (Public Broadcasting System). Thus, WACB was an organization of members who supported their Christian-oriented and church-related professional association, functioning as a kind of lobby in public networks.

In the 1970s there was still some competition about the primacy of print over electronic media. So there was then the question who should lead the new WACC because of a mixture of competing interests. Its first president was Christopher Kolade, the former director general of Nigerian broadcasting and future Nigerian High Commissioner to the United Kingdom. I followed Dr. Philip Johnson as general secretary of WACC. I had neither a print nor electronic media background, but I happened to be available after the merger of PCWM and PWMD in Hamburg. One of my first contributions to WACC was to keep the CLF dowry in reserve for the possibility of an emergency during which, at some undetermined future, the WACC would be closed down; its staff needed to be adequately provisioned for an inevitable redundancy. According to my latest information this dowry is still untouched.

When in January 1976 I came to London, WACC's office was in a flat on the second floor of what had been a residential building in St. James' Street, two houses to the north of what had been the Texas embassy to the Court of St. James between 1836 and 1845. The staff more than filled the flat. My desk was part of the lobby in front of the flat, probably seen as a safe place for the newcomer from Hamburg.

My arrival from Hamburg was similar to the shock of coming from the hinterland to the metropolis. The streets were full of people and traffic; colleagues were made up of people from Asia, Scandinavia, and ex-British colonial officers; and I had to relate to a network of social contacts with which I was not comfortable. I imagine that Philip Johnson, my predecessor from the information staff of Franklin Clark Fry's Lutheran Church in America in New York City, much better met the social expectations of a WACC general secretary than I did.

The BBC religious broadcasting people meant to smooth my way into London life. One day early on, a gentleman came to my desk in front of the flat and suggested I employ the services of a young secretary, a Lady Seymour, related to the Blues and Royals with personal access to the royal stables, in order to have a happy exposure to what London had to offer. Lady Seymour, young and racy indeed, came to the office and offered to work for WACC three or so days a week; for the rest of it, we could have lots of fun. By not taking that opportunity I missed my acculturation into British life.

WACC's presence on St. James's Street was short-lived. In the summer of 1976 Brian, the WACC comptroller—whom I inherited—found a two-story bridge office across from the Sainsbury forecourt in Kings Road. Brian, an ex-colonial administrator in Africa, was as helpful as he was charming and entertaining. His elephant hunting stories and sherries before lunch were enjoyed by all. However, the WACC budget for the first year did not get beyond the back of an envelope. I must say, his charm captivated young ladies in the office and from WACC committees. When he was persuaded to leave, we all felt that an amusing piece of furniture was missing.

Bertie Emmanuel, an Anglican priest from India, and Neville Jayaweera, the former director general of Sri Lanka Broadcasting, were the directors of Print and Electronic Media. They were the stable and reliable backbone of WACC. Through Bertie, WACC obtained the experience and editorial capacity of Dr. Michael Traber, a Swiss Roman Catholic missionary priest from Zambia and Zimbabwe.

Mike and his young associate, Philip Lee, repatriated an old WACB journal from Frankfurt and rejuvenated it into *Media Development*, the professional WACC quarterly. It is, still with Philip Lee as its editor, a respected, multilingual journal which reflects the intellectual evolution of increasingly relevant indigenous views and topics of religious aspects in communication and politics.

Neville represented WACC at the BBC committee on religious broadcasting and was a member of the committee which directed the United Nations Education Scientific and Cultural Organization (UNESCO) Department of Development and Research under the chairmanship of Sean MacBride. Neville's concise and brilliant lectures in many parts of the world have been appreciated by many professionals. One of his unforgettable sayings in conjunction with the quality and/or administration of electronic media projects was: "Lousy administration, whether in Africa or Asia, remains lousy administration, and cannot be tolerated!"

Among the staff I inherited was the Rev. Ronald Englund, a former American missionary to Tanzania. He looked after the WACC newsletter, the monthly communication with WACC's membership around the world. On Sundays, Ron often had afternoon Swahili services for African students in St. Ann's Lutheran Church in East London. When I left, the newsletter was edited by Ann Shakespeare, a former Royal Navy recruitment officer.

One area of involvement was women's communication. During my first WACC Central Committee (CentComm) on Malta in May 1976, WACC was urgently challenged to do more for training and supporting women in third world papers, journals, and radio stations. An academic communications expert, Margaret Gallagher, impressed CentComm with knowledge and conviction and had been hired as a permanent staff executive in this field. In 1976 CentComm passed a recommendation that the wide field of women in communication and communication by women should become a firmly funded aspect of WACC's ministry. I consider this an important addition and like to think that this must be one of the results not only of Margaret Gallagher's communication, but also of the round-the-clock prayers of Roman Catholic nuns of a silent convent on Malta. Father Bennie, on behalf of the Roman Catholic Archbishop of Malta, had diligently and successfully prepared the logistics for this CentComm meeting, informing us only after its conclusion of the praying nuns of Malta. Eventually a Roman Catholic religious from the Philippines, Terri Amano, directed this portfolio of WACC's ministry to remarkable respect and success.

Once the delicate merger of CLF and WACB had matured into an international and professional membership, the task of securing the annual income for the multimedia training and production projects, the support of which was requested from WACC, became the new challenge. Its personal and corporate membership fees never came close to the growing funding expectations. At best they came to between four and seven percent of WACC's annual budget. My past association with LWF and WCC funding allowed me to cultivate the same or similar funding agencies which had stood so successfully behind the ecumenical project needs in Geneva. Most of these agencies were of course church-related. The challenge of approaching these agencies was to convince them that WACC projects had as sound an ecumenical provenance to be funded as those for which support is requested by the LWF or WCC. A greater challenge was the hurdle to accept that communication training and production projects were as vital for indigenous development as drilling for water or building a hospital in Africa. Enabling people in these countries to make their views on their realities known to the world at large is indeed comparable to helping with water or medicine. And—as I discovered during my Ph.D. research—the view of indigenous Christians is practically identical to the political views and social expectations of their non-Christian neighbors. Thus, communication is a vital dimension of human rights, and enabling such communication to become internationally understood and accepted, especially in the West, is a legitimate Christian contribution to development—the development to communicate in freedom and with confidence.

The funding partners of WACC, which shared this attitude, were such church-related development agencies as the Dutch Inter-church Organization for Development Cooperation (ICCO), Swiss Bread for Brothers, Scandinavian church and national development agencies, the German Churches' Central Development Aid, and my former Hamburg PCWM. In PCWM it was especially Frank Kuerschner who for many years managed PCWM's annual WACC support portfolio with great understanding and unerring commitment.

Through its international membership and WACC's commitment for nurturing the indigenous view in communication, it was not long before the World Association for Christian Communication became the global conglomerate of its regional associations. The first among them was the European association, carrying forward a European professional entity from its WACB beginnings. Similarly, the American Association of Christian Broadcasters (AACB) came into being. The AACB was interesting in that it maintained very close relations to the radio group association of the American Roman Catholic Bishops' Conference. These groups met annually during the first week after the U.S. Thanksgiving in Fort Lauderdale, Florida. This time and place was cherished because of the Florida climate; in the north of the U.S. and Canada it often was already winter-like and cold. The AACB Florida meetings maintained through the years its unique daily schedule: 8:00-11:00 a.m.–worship and lectures, 11:00 a.m.-4:00 p.m.–beach time, 4:00-10:00 p.m.–lectures, seminars, and after-dinner television and film samples of productions by the joint membership.

My first attendance was perhaps in 1977. After meetings in Chicago I came late to Ft. Lauderdale. I was met by Chuck, a Roman Catholic radio producer, and Murri, the Munich assistant to WACC's treasurer, Dr. Geisendorfer. After check-in, I was lost in the big hotel lobby. Dinner was about to end. A few people drifted by, but I didn't know any of them. A striking Jane Fonda-type woman came across to me: "You must be Dr. Florin. Come with me." I ended up on the balcony of the Roman Catholic conference suite. The Fonda look-alike asked two young ladies to look after me. Over a glass of bourbon I learned that these young ladies were Roman Catholic nuns working in a Catholic TV studio in Hollywood. This year was the first in which their order had allowed a more informal dress code. Together we admired a full moon reflection stretching eastwards over the black Atlantic.

Munich Murri, the secretary of WACC Europe, had a similar surprise. After the close of the AACB conference, the Roman Catholic group had its annual prize presentation dinner for its media productions. As WACC guests, Murri and I had our places at the head table. The room filled slowly with Roman Catholic producers, writers, directors, and camera people—many in formal clergy and habit gear. Quite surprised and impressed by this formal attire, Murri whispered, "Look at all these gorgeous young men from the beach now in dog collars. I am glad that I have been a good girl!"

As the years went on, the AACB split into a North American and Latin American Association for Christian Communication. Not much later there followed Asian and Pacific associations. At the inauguration of the Pacific Association for Christian Communication (PACC) on Fiji, I was to give the opening address. As happened so often, I delayed my departure from the London office to the last possible moment. On arrival in Fiji via Sydney, my body clock was twelve hours out of time. I arrived in late afternoon on the day on which, after dinner, my address was due. The jet lag distortion was so complete that I could not form a single cohesive sentence. With my deepest apologies, I asked to reschedule my remarks for the next morning. This was my first twelve-hour jet lag experience with little sleep between evening and morning. The inauguration itself proceeded well. I became convinced that there was a difference between the world of Asia and the world of the Pacific including Australia and New Zealand. At first I had hesitated to go for yet another regional association and the costs this would incur for the WACC budget. But if WACC's policy of enabling an authentic indigenous voice in the concert of the multi-voiced choir of humanity was to be taken seriously, then PACC certainly had a reason to exist. This was underlined in Fijian style at the concluding event, sharing in community the slightly toxic drink of kava root powder and water. I was ordered the head place in this lively circle of new friends, with men forming the inner circle and women the outer circle. Why? I don't know, it was not explained. But that I should have the head place, called "Numba One," was explained with smirk and laughter, the details of which every Pacific native would understand.

The other local context of a regional association meeting was that of the Latin American Regional Association for Christian Communication (LARACC) in Brazil. WACC London was represented by Thelma Awori, staff executive for the Women in Communication desk, an absolutely competent Liberian lady who had fled Uganda with her children in a VW Beetle non-stop to Nairobi after her Kampala neighbor, Idi Amin, had, through an officer of his guard, let her know that he was personally very interested in her. After her time with WACC, Thelma became the U.N. Commissioner for Zimbabwe in Harare.

On the long night flight to Rio de Janeiro it dawned on us that we should stay in Rio for a day and take in the fabulous Rio carnival parade. We called LARACC's chairman, Hilmar Kannenberg, in Novo Hamburgo and asked for permission: "No way! You would get lost in Rio. But you won't miss Carnival. We have a carnival parade in Novo Hamburgo. Get on your flight. I'll pick you up at Porto Alegre."

Carnival in Rio must be a physically stressful time! In the Rio airport telephone exchange we found a sparsely clad young lady deeply asleep across her desk. It took a while to get her to connect us with Novo Hamburgo, but by the time we got there, we were heavily fortified with several caipirinhas and needed a restful pre-parade relaxation at Hilmar's swimming pool. The Novo Hamburgo carnival parade came off with local aplomb. As visitors from abroad we had the mayor between us, who noted that I was a citizen of Hamburg, Germany—but he was more interested in my WACC colleague Thelma Awori. At the Novo Hamburgo swimming pool, I met Iria, Hilmar's secretary, who later was for a short time my secretary in London. She then married an English businessman, the Latin American American Express (AMEX) coordinator in Rio.

Through the lively interaction of the regional associations with the WACC office in London, the policy position of WACC became known in the world of communication—a process which helped greatly to stabilize WACC as a professional partner in the wide field of religious communication.

An important policy development grew out of the experience of our North American colleagues with the emergence of the electronic church. Huge, interdenominational radio and TV ministries attracted lapsed, lost, or secularized Christians with a privilege-affirming message of the gospel of affluence. It was so easy to accept a lifestyle which justified the comfort of "consume" as fulfilment of a personal faith in Jesus, the sweet Shepherd. In the work of WACC's staff and committees, we felt ever more estranged from such persuasive displays of the certainties of the Christian faith. In its regions and by its projects in training and message outreach, WACC attempted a different style of Christian discipleship. During this time there were a few approaches by one or two big-name electronic evangelists about cooperation or membership, but none ever came close to any form of association, much less to any support from these incredibly well-endowed institutions.

The closest link to any outside contact grew with UNESCO. Sean MacBride's book *Many Voices, One World* provided the base for UNESCO's New World Information and Communication Order (NWICO). This policy challenged particularly the West and its dominant news agencies such as Reuters, Voice of America, Radio Moscow, and Deutsche Presse Agentur. These agencies had become accustomed to telling the world what was happening around the planet, then interpreting the events in order to come to "correct conclusions" in understanding what was going on. Often, the smaller non-Western news media felt insulted concerning the interpretation of events in their own backyards: "Much of what the big ones say about us is wrong. Why can't we tell the world of our own events with our own interpretations, thus striving for a fairer and more just global communication order?" When NWICO became the policy of UNESCO, the big news agencies of the West (Reuters, Agence France Press and ABC, CBS, and NBC of America) persuaded their governments to stop their statutory annual contributions to the UNESCO budget. An otherwise unrecognized crisis among world media was the result.

I can't remember whether NWICO was the trigger to approach Sean MacBride to become a member of the WACC Central Committee, but the fact is that he accepted the invitation. After Namibia's independence, the United Nations Organization (UNO) appointed Sean MacBride to chair the UNESCO Committee for Research and Development in Paris. Prior to his responsibilities in Namibia, Sean MacBride had been the foreign secretary of the Republic of Ireland. He has reported that he was the first Irish foreign secretary who spoke English with a French accent—his mother had to flee to France with her children after the 1916 Irish uprising because his father, a committed Republican, was captured, tried, condemned, shot, and made a martyr of the Irish Republic. MacBride grew up in Paris with a French education.

After MacBride accepted his membership in the WACC Central Committee, he came once to our London office to address the staff and discuss the thinking behind the NWICO policy with us. He started with the insight that communication technology, like most other technologies, outruns the social, moral, and ethical development of humankind; they are dictated in their speed of development by the greed of industry and the "requirements" of the market. And, regarding these "requirements," it is the use which technology producers make of an ever-more rapidly spreading communication to persuade the consumer of the validity which the market, the secular mystique of modernity, requires.

Sean MacBride illustrated this insight with his proverbial story which I have often retold myself. The news which the world absorbs daily is condensed by a handful of mass media. The majority of daily local press media either ignores the wide flow of information or picks its most spectacular portions for a one-paragraph comment, preferably with a picture. The sad consequence of this practice is that in the powerful industrialized countries, the daily consumers of this reduced input live in democracies which entitle them to vote. The alternatives available to be voted on are determined by the natural desire of politicians to secure yet another period in office. And these alternatives are rarely ever critical enough to endanger re-election. In the interest of an industrialized market, the producers of desirable consumables often financially support such politicians whose electoral programs most likely secure the stability of the market.

In our discussions we came up with a question of whether the democratic principle itself had outlived the shelf life of our present markets. "Not at all." Sean MacBride upheld the idea of democracy, but added that the voters have to be better informed and then demonstrate publicly in streets and places their reason for a fair, just, and peaceful world. As I remember MacBride's visit to the WACC office in the early 1980s, I now, writing these memories in 2012, understand better what MacBride shared with us then. If Sean MacBride were still alive today, he would see in the ups and downs of the Arab Spring the necessary birth pains of a brighter future.

He left us that day, over a generation ago, with a simple and rural story in words I cannot quote verbatim because our WACC conference room was not equipped for recording the proceedings of that day. However, the story went something like this: There is this farmer in Tanzania. When he leaves his *rondavel* in the morning he takes his transistor shortwave radio with him. Attending his fields he listens to the Swahili programs—news and interpretations of BBC World Service, Radio Moscow, Deutsche Welle, Voice of America, and his Tanzanian Broadcasting System. Much of what he hears refers to the same world events, but they are interpreted and analyzed quite differently, if not contrasted beyond comparison. MacBride ended with this question: Who do you think understands more of what is going on in this world—the Tanzanian farmer or a Western consumer of mass circulation newspapers? And the sad thing is that those consumers have the vote!

UNESCO quite realistically recognized that without a major portion of statutory support of its budget, it didn't have a chance to survive. This would put UNESCO's main responsibilities for education, science, and a balanced future for children in danger. Without much publicity, UNESCO dropped the active pursuit of its NWICO policy and enquired through its research and development committee member, Neville Jayaweera, WACC's director of electronic media projects, whether WACC would continue the concerns of the NWICO policy with a low profile. Behind this informal inquiry was UNESCO's appreciation of WACC's policy for a fair and just communication right for all. And with low profile it was that WACC kept this concern alive—a concern which was widely shared among its members and particularly by the editorial board of its quarterly, *Media Development*.

It was in the days of the first half of the 1980s that an unannounced man appeared in the reception space of our two-story bridge office. This man flicked through some WACC information brochures on display and was apparently in no hurry to ask for any specific staff officer. This caused the receptionist, a small Greek Cypriot woman, to call and have me come down quickly. There he was, a tall full-sized man with trench coat and a self-assured American accent. To my question, "Can I help you?" he had this to say: "No thank you. Nothing for the moment. Just looking around. For now we consider you as friends—and I trust it will stay that way!" And he left! Who was this man? He didn't fit the image of a hobo reconnoitering for a secure break-in and a warm night after dark. No more information was revealed when I kicked this around with some of my staff. All that remained was a rather curious question mark.

Like Klaus Vieweger in Hamburg, Thelma Awori organized for WACC Women in Media show and tell trips to some of our projects. Thelma insisted that I, as WACC general secretary, had to be with her on the first trip to Beirut. There were twelve or so powerful ladies, media professionals all, and one young Greek Orthodox divinity student, Angelos Vellipotes, who had her secondary education in the Wilhelm Doerpfeld Gymnasium in Athens (likenamed to my secondary school in the 1940s in Wuppertal). Her German was perfect. She worked in Greek National Radio religious broadcasting.

Why should I, as the only male, get involved in this trip? Thelma pleaded with me: "But you have to come along. You are the WACC. Besides, you have been to Beirut several times before!" As Thelma is a lady who does not accept no for an answer, I was on my way to Lebanon. Innocently I had booked a hotel I had stayed in earlier and suggested visits to the Near East Council of Churches (NECC) with its general secretary, Gabi Habib, to its radio studio in the Near East School of Theology (NEST), to the Catholicos of the West Armenian Orthodox Church in Antelias near Beirut, and to Byblos, an old Phoenician harbor and the source from which many Western letter types evolved: Egyptian hieroglyphics, Phoenician cuneiform, Greek, Hebrew, Arabic, and Roman.

After our visit to Antelias, one forceful American journalist zeroed in on me: "Why did you have to introduce us individually to the Catholicos? We are strong professional women and well able to introduce ourselves. Just stay out of our way." Such feminist onslaught was completely new to me, as it was to the young Greek student Angelos, and I tried to stand aside as much as I could from them. Still, several times there were less vivid reminders to keep quiet, as when meeting old ecumenical friends again like Gabi Habib or the rector of NEST. Over the last supper at our hotel, one more matronly type came to my table to explain once more that women now lived in a new liberated age, free of any patronizing male influence. Yes, this WACC Women in the Media encounter was a not forgotten lesson—and I never joined another trip!

This would have been all, had it not been for a very noisy event at midnight. I couldn't believe my ears. Never since the war had I come across such intensive machine gun fire as that which was going on outside the hotel. Before I knew what was going on, women drummed at my door and burst in: "Hans, what is this? You have to do something. You have to make them stop." My advice was to hide by the inside brick wall below the window sill, suggesting this as the safest place from any bullets through the window panes. Then I called reception to find out what was going on. "Nothing to worry about. Sorry for the disturbance. Today is the Prophet's birthday and in this general political unrest, we have not got any firecrackers, so our machine guns will have to do! Go to bed and sleep safely."

Our last breakfast the next morning was a very quiet affair!

My WACC contract was open-ended. However, after WACC had grown into a stable and recognized agency, I began to realize that now WACC should be led by a communications professional. Around that time I received a call from Bishop Lohse, the chairman of the EKD Council and president of the United Bible Societies (UBS). Would I be interested in becoming the UBS Secretary for Europe and the Near East? This prospect was a great temptation; but one cannot just drop and leave WACC, a well-functioning ecumenical institution. On the other hand, one cannot simply disregard an invitation from the presiding EKD bishop, who after all was my ultimate "warlord." So, I agreed to take on this job. This change would not be as strange as taking on WACC had been, because for some years I had chaired the committee which oversaw this region. Besides, I could not leave WACC immediately. The UBS was prepared to wait for a while. It took almost a year until my successor, the Rev. Carlos Valle, head of a Protestant radio studio in Buenos Aires, was able to take over the helm at WACC.

United Bible Societies
Regional Secretary of Europe and the Near East
1986-1991

My joining the UBS was like a homecoming. After my years as chair of European Regional Executive Committee (EUREC), I knew the regional center and its staff knew me. Likewise I was familiar with a number of the challenges in the region—not least among them the problems associated with Bible work behind the Iron Curtain. This curtain had been of particular interest to my predecessor, Svere Smaadahl, a Norwegian Lutheran pastor, who had experience in clandestine cross border traffic between Nazi-occupied Norway and neutral Sweden. Svere had discovered early that it was best to travel behind the Iron Curtain with valid visas and official invitations from our Bible partners in Eastern Europe. It was Svere who had enlisted the early regional staff: Peter Wigglesworth, Paul Fueter, and Dr. Jan de Waard, the regional translation consultant. By the time I joined UBS, there were additional experts on board: Terje Hartberg (admininstration), Dr. Manuel Jimbashian (translation), Erwin Zimmermann (print and publishing), consultants all. Regarding working in Eastern Europe, all were following Svere's policy—a policy which had emerged from a EUREC meeting in Bad Saarow in the German Democratic Republic in 1973. It was then that Svere, as regional secretary, and I as EUREC chair, concurred with the policy that was later adopted by all the

United Bible Societies, that in order to facilitate Bible work behind the Iron Curtain, UBS would negotiate directly with the authorities about production in and Scripture imports to their respective countries. Between 1973 and 1986, work in Eastern Europe had seen a slow but steady progress. All regional staff became acquainted with the delicacies of this work. And when I joined in 1986 I could fully rely on my staff, who knew how to pursue the tasks on which we had agreed to work. During the time of General Secretary Gorbachev's policy of *glasnost*, the Iron Curtain became more porous. The reliability of my staff and the increasing possibilities of access to Eastern Europe contributed to the fact that my time with UBS became one of the most fascinating work opportunities of my professional working life!

However, before relating some of the details of my experiences in this amazing time, I want to preserve for my memory two of my thoughts on Bible work—the relation of the Bible to my faith and the Bible smugglers.

1. The relation of the Bible to my faith: I remember quite vividly that, when in 1970 Baron van Tuyll came to my hospital bed in Hamburg to ask whether I would like to follow him in the EUREC chairmanship, I hesitated in my response. I cannot share the enthusiasm for mass production and distribution of the Bible around the world, because I see Bible work similarly motivated by Christ's all-inclusive mission command to teach and baptize all nations, as the fathers of World Mission were enthusiastic in the nineteenth century to follow this call. Yes, the Bible is the Word of God. But God has not dictated God's Word. To me the Bible retells the many different and sometimes contradictory experiences of people who believe in God—first in Yahweh, the God of Israel, and later in God, Father, Son, and Holy Spirit. Likewise, the New Testament was not written by Jesus, the Son of God, but by named evangelists, who had heard of Jesus and had come to believe in him. And then there was the Apostle Paul, first a learned fanatic until, touched by Christ, he became Christ's first

transcultural missionary whose letters precede the Gospels in time. And again, yes, this so diverse and multifaceted collection of human experiences of God is indeed the Word of God—but a Word I cannot follow blindly and fanatically. By the time I had come up with these thoughts—not as condensed or cohesive as those above—we had drunk some cups of tea. The baron's reply was short and simple: "I can understand your view, and it is exactly the view we need in the UBS in Europe." After the baron had left I somehow knew that I could be of help to EUREC.

2. The world of Bible smuggling is a post-World War II phenomenon. The UBS wouldn't exist if there had not been generations of faithful Christians, especially in Europe and North America, who treasured Holy Scripture as the Word of God. We know that the Bible movement had its beginnings in the nineteenth century when the Christian response to Christ's mission command began to extend to all nations. Travel beyond the Christian occident became safer and easier. Missionaries and Bible colporteurs shared the inner calling to make known the Word of God throughout the world.

In the Bible, especially in the Old Testament, God's people were encircled by enemies, often condemned to destruction by God's prophets. Subconsciously this seeming God obedience was kept alive during the wars of the nineteenth and twentieth centuries when nations assured their armies that it was God's will to defeat and destroy their enemies. Since the fourth century, kings and emperors fought their wars under the sign of Christ's cross or with belt buckles in the name of Immanuel—*Gott mit uns*/God with us. When, after World War II, communism continued to be the predominant ideology in the Soviet Union, the "Christian" West had a new enemy which in "God's name" it could defile, condemn, and if possible defeat. Particularly conservative Christians, who recognized in the Word of God the divine tool with which to undermine the perceived anti-Christian ideology of communism, took the Soviet prohibition of the Bible as justification for smuggling Holy Scriptures into Soviet-dominated Eastern Europe. Not without danger to themselves, Bible smugglers bypassed any contact with the authorities in order to get Bibles to isolated Christians behind the Iron Curtain. In conservative evangelical circles these smugglers became admired heroes of God-pleasing anti-communism. The UBS policy of negotiated Scripture imports was condemned as collaboration with the enemy. Not only had such rejection become detrimental to UBS support from politically conservative Christians, but these smuggling operations began to endanger the churches which they intended to help! Thus, it is no wonder that the UBS regional staff had become unhappy with Bible smuggling, and I soon learned to share this unhappiness. And it did not come as a surprise that a UBS colleague in East Berlin had heard of shelves of Bibles in West Berlin's antiquarian bookstores which had been left behind by people prior to crossing via Friedrichstrasse or Checkpoint Charlie. It is with this attitude that I began my work in the UBS regional center for Europe and the Near East (including North Africa).

For my approaches to Bible work in Eastern Europe, it was my conviction that it was important to start with the majority church in any country. In Eastern Europe these were often the autonomous Orthodox churches, which traditionally had released Bible access to the clergy. The laity received Holy Scripture through lectionary readings during the liturgy. This custom, shared by the Roman Catholic Church until Vatican I (1870), was still the rule in orthodoxy. The challenge for lay access to the Bible came through communism and its widely extended education and high level of literacy which motivated lay people to read the Bible, a book guarded by the church and ideologically prohibited by the state.

In my staff it became the norm to seek Orthodox contact through influential church leaders—a practice found especially useful by the regional translation consultants.

It was in this context that I made my first contact in the USSR with Metropolitan Pitirim, bishop of Volokolamsk and director of the Orthodox publishing house at the Russian Patriarchate in Moscow. I knew Metropolitan Pitirim from my work in WACC. The European regional association of WACC once had a meeting, arranged by Pitirim, in Moscow. This included a bus excursion to Volokolamsk, the western-most outpost of Moscow, from which one could reach downtown Moscow by tram, and where, in December 1941, the German invasion had come to a stop. The bus stopped outside Volokolamsk where police had a few words with the bishop. We learned that our august group of international communicators would enter the town under police protection complete with blue flashing lights. Our regional meeting, the first for WACC in Russia, ended with a toast to the spirit of Volokolamsk and the promise of lasting Europe-wide Christian communication.

In memory of this event, I contacted Metropolitan Pitirim and asked for a visit to discuss how the old and defunct Russian Bible Society could be resurrected. The reunion with Pitirim was great, but my request for a Bible society was not as successful. That name would be too mindful of the original Russian Bible Society under tsarist patronage. Besides, an unlimited number of Bibles in the still intact USSR needed a lot of internal discussion. Was it not the Bible which convinced Martin Luther to become a heretic? Even up to the present, "Lutheran" is a generic term for heretic in Russian. "But let's keep in touch." Could there be a way?!

A few months later I received an invitation from the Metropolitan. Come to Moscow, and he would book a flight for me to Tbilisi in Georgia where I should talk to Ilia II, the Georgian Orthodox patriarch, about a Georgian Bible Society. If Ilia II liked the idea, perhaps something could be done in Moscow. I flew to Tbilisi with one of Pitirim's publishing executives—in a double decker Aeroflot of course. We were met by a fluent English speaker, a young reserve lieutenant of the Red Army. We were encouraged to rest a bit, have dinner with good Georgian wine, and then go to the opera for Tchaikovsky's *Eugene Onegin*. "Tomorrow we shall see the patriarch."

Patriarch Ilia II liked the idea of a Georgian Bible Society in principle. That such a Bible society would be interdenominational should not be a problem in this ecumenical age. Might it not perhaps be possible, he asked, to think also of an Armenian Bible Society? "Our churches are probably the oldest uninterrupted churches in Christendom, from the fourth and fifth centuries."

Back in Moscow that was noted with interest: "We shall see. And before you leave you should have a word with the director of the Department of Religion, directly linked to the Ministerial Council, the highest organ in the USSR. This visit would make future trips to Russia much easier!" And an interesting visit it was indeed. I met the director, without a tie and wearing an open corduroy jacket, in a simple office, sitting at a plain table. We spoke in German; he was absolutely fluent. "So, you would like to see another Bible Society in Russia?" Yes, if possible. "But if yes, then it must be without any resemblance to the former tsarist patronage!" I learned that the Soviet Department of Religion was the continuation of the religious directorate of Ivan the Great's government after that tsar had dissolved the Russian Orthodox patriarchate in Moscow, because the influence of the Russian Orthodox Church had stayed too far behind the times! And again the director said: "By the way, it was the USSR government which reinstated the Moscow patriarchate in 1918—one of its first decrees!" Any later visa applications to the USSR embassy in London were quickly forthcoming.

Two further trips to the USSR followed soon—one to Tbilisi with Dr. Jan de Waard, by then the regional translations coordinator, and the other to Yerevan, the capital of the then still Soviet Republic of Armenia, which had requested its integration in the mid-1920s as protection against territorial interests of Turkey and Azerbaijan. On the trip to Yerevan, I was accompanied by my Armenian translation consultant, Dr. Manuel Jimbashian and by Erwin Zimmermann, the competent consultant in print and production techniques.

In Tbilisi the idea of a Georgian Bible Society was not any more the big issue. In time there would be a society. But could the UBS in the meantime assist in the revision of the old Georgian Bible? This request was indeed interesting. A revision of the Russian standard Bible of the 1880s, the follow-up to the old church Slavonic texts, linguistically had become desirable, but the church was politically not yet prepared to discuss it. As far as I can remember the old Georgian text was not comparable to the church's Slavonic text of the old Russian Bible, but it was incomprehensible to literates of the twentieth century. For the old Georgian Bible revision, Jan de Waard found linguistic interest in the Georgian Academy of Sciences and support from the UBS regional budget. The Russian revision of the 1880s in Pushkin's neo-Russian was another matter. In the Russian Orthodox liturgy, the Slavonic text was still heard but not understood, and the 1880s text needed to be rejuvenated by a new translation. But the Russian metropolitans and the patriarch considered a modern translation out of the question. I did regret this attitude very much. If modern Russian in the late twentieth century had deteriorated as much as the political German of the GDR, then a serious revision of the Russian Bible should by now be on the way!

In Yerevan the situation was quite different from that in Georgia. The Catholicos, the head of the Armenian Orthodox Church, does not live in Yerevan but in a monastery campus called Etchmiadzin, half an hour's drive out of the capital, directly on the Turkish border. Manuel Jimbashian and I had our rooms on the campus. Manuel, who had been there before, introduced me to the eighty-year-old Catholicos. With a warm-hearted smile and in fluent German, he welcomed me and explained that he had his secondary education in the classics German Grammar School in Bucharest, Romania. Yes, it would be very helpful indeed if the UBS could help his church upgrade a bookshop on the campus into an Armenian Bible Society and help with equipping a printery into a Bible printing press, once Manuel and his colleagues completed their revision of the old Armenian Bible. This, roughly, was the topic of our one-hour conversation. After lunch Manuel showed me the campus garden. For the evening the Catholicos invited us to a concert in Yerevan: Would we join him at his car after sunset?

The leisurely walk through the garden included the inspection of the rocky grave-pit of St. Gregory the Great Illuminator, creator of one of the oldest Armenian Bible manuscripts of the fourth century. Equally fascinating was the barbed wire fortified garden gate, behind which was Turkish territory. Far in the west in the light of the fading sun one could make out among the deep reach of hills in Turkey the top of Mount Ararat. Legend has it that after the Great Flood, Noah's ark first touched ground and settled down there. In the museum of the monastery, we were later shown the rudder and anchor of the ark—the sacred proof that Noah's family clan, with all their animals, wild and tame, had multiplied from that spot of antiquity.

The concert in Yerevan is one of the most moving experiences of my life. The ride with the Catholicos in his German government black Mercedes was uninterrupted until it came to a sedate stop amid an open space in front of the opera full of people. As the car doors opened, the place fell quiet. Manuel and I followed His Holiness through the crowds. Most people bowed their heads and crossed themselves in recognition of their much-beloved Catholicos. On the way we saw how women just touched his flowing robe. At the bottom of the stairs the opera director welcomed this august party and explained to Manuel that the Khachaturian concert this evening would open with the old patriarchal hymn, last heard in 1910.

When we followed the Catholicos into the upper first row honor box, the audience and orchestra rose, bowed and remained standing through the length of the hymn. For the first time, so we were told, the Armenian National Orchestra played that evening under the wide sway of the future national flag: light blue, white, and black.

On the way back to the monastery the Catholicos explained that he had not known that he would be honored with the patriarchal hymn, and that he could not stop tears flowing down his cheeks. We ourselves were not far from such emotional response.

With the UBS I had one more trip to Armenia, again with Manuel. This time there were complications: A nuclear reactor in the Armenian hinterland had suffered an accident, and power had become very scarce. The objective this time was to meet with the faculty of the theological seminary in Yerevan. As this seminary also served the minority churches in Armenia, particularly Baptists, it was our intention to find lines of contact through seminary lecturers to the leaders of the minority churches. Two topics were on our agenda: the level of interest in cooperating with an ecumenical Bible society and professional input into a revision, if not an outright modern translation, of the traditional Armenian Bible. There were some surprised, raised eyebrows: Do you really expect full ecumenical cooperation in an Armenian Bible Society? Yes, we would, and yes, such was the UBS policy. The result was cautious interest, but not yet much optimism. I realized that the way to an Armenian Bible Society and a revision or newly translated Bible would extend over a good number of years. Perhaps I should not have expected more, because the classic jokes of "Radio Yerevan" came to mind, which characterized Russian backwardness to this culturally and historically remote edge of the Soviet Union. (With the initial framework established, a full Armenian Bible Society became a reality after my retirement.)

The shortage of power (electrical power blackout) during this visit had two results: I could leave Yerevan early for Kishinev in Moldova, and on the last morning in the monastery I had a very cold shower without a shave. The bathroom mirror reflected only a 4:00 a.m. early pre-dawn glimmer of daylight.

The flight across Georgia and along the eastern shore of the Black Sea in a crowded Aeroflot plane was rewarded by some beautiful sights below, but was otherwise uneventful. It is Russian custom that once a plane has come to a stand-still, one gets up, collects masses of hand luggage, fills the aisles, and works hard to get off. All this happened in Kishinev—except there was no movement in the aisles. Only slowly was I able to figure out that the loudspeaker repeated with increasing irritation, "Gospodin Florina, Gospodin Florina." I grabbed my carry-on, squeezed through the crowded aisles, and realized that an Orthodox priest in a flowing robe and impressive black cowl stood at the bottom of the stairs.

In seconds we were in a black car, swung around the plane, and rushed across the tarmac in the direction of downtown Kishinev, the capital of Moldova, a province which Stalin had sliced off Romania in the 1940s. Terje Hartberg, my administrative colleague from the regional center, had not yet arrived. He was expected later that night. Together we would have the opportunity to explore what chances there were for a Moldovan Bible Society and whether the UBS could help with logistics in Scripture production and distribution. Terje, a gifted negotiator, was the right man for making our story in Kishinev a success, just as he had been through the years in the USSR. The next day Erwin Zimmermann, our print and publishing consultant, joined us after a somewhat complicated overnight train ride from Bucharest, Romania. What did a German, coming from Romania, have in mind? The suspicions were greater among the USSR border personnel than on the Romanian side.

Having missed a real shower and shave in the morning, I had just turned on the hot tap in my hotel when I heard impressive knocks at the door. Bare as I was, I found the Orthodox priest outside. He hurried me: "Quick, get dressed and pack your bag. You are in the wrong hotel!" On the way around the block I learned that only a few days before, the city party chief had offered the Metropolitan use of the government guesthouse and that I would be the guinea pig for trying it out. On the steps of the guesthouse, a well-endowed Russian matron welcomed us and showed us to "my" flat. This flat had more floor space than my cottage in Sidlesham. It had parquet flooring; a generous lobby; a big bathroom with tub, shower, and bidet; a conference room for eight with with cut glass sets for eight for sherry, brandy, vodka, whisky, white and red wine; a kitchen; and a simply huge bedroom. The priest looked around and murmured, more to himself, "So that is how the party elite lives; no wonder they are corrupt." To me he said, "I'll pick you up in one hour for lunch!"

When Terje arrived late at night, he was as surprised as I had been. The breakfast, which the matron handled personally, was ample—with bacon, borscht, and eggs. The matron informed us that around 10:00 a.m. seven churchmen, Orthodox and others, would come. We could have the conference room to ourselves, and she would stand by for coffee or tea as we would wish.

The conference was very similar to that in Yerevan. They were curious what the UBS had to offer, doubtfully surprised whether a Bible society could become reality, and Bible printing and translation help was very much welcome. This program was very much like what the UBS was already doing for churches in Romania.

By noon Erwin Zimmermann had arrived. The afternoon was divided into visits to a temporary Bible depot, a print shop, and churches for talks with local leaders of non-Orthodox denominations. The next morning we were shown Kishinev, a bourgeois town, a mix of Mediterranean and Austro-Hungarian beauty.

The unforgettable Moldovan event followed in the afternoon. In a VW Kombi, the priest drove us into the hinterland to what he was sure would be a surprise for us. In a factory forecourt we changed from the Kombi into a pre-war Skoda Tatra, a good-sized black luxury limousine, the likes of which none of us had ever seen. But the car was not the surprise. This unfolded when the Tatra approached a big gate, moving into a tunnel behind the factory. Once inside the mountain, further tunnels split off to the left and right, all stocked with huge wine barrels. This, so the priest explained, is the biggest vineyard in Moldova, and its manager would be very grateful if we could recommend this wine to a supermarket chain in the West.

After cruising through the tunnels for some twenty minutes, we came to a big barrel, standing. We all got out of the Tatra when the barrel's front split into two equal halves. This was the entrance into a huge, cathedral-like space inside the mountain at one side of which, next to a live fireplace, a dinner table was decked out. We found our places in very comfortable leather armchairs and were treated to a superb wine-tasting accompanied by delicious, freshly broiled steaks. Tastes and varieties matched easily, if not favorably, with what I knew about wine. Terje suggested that bottle labels might reflect a more romantic ambience for Western marketing. I promised I would alert Tim Sainsbury to this treasure of wine. Within two to three weeks after Kishinev I talked with Tim Sainsbury, for whom I chaired a communication projects funding committee. "Interesting," was his reply, "but thank you, no." Sainsbury's have their own wine merchants who know best. Because this was the last I had heard on this matter, I took it that I had failed the manager of the biggest vineyard in Moldova. This may have been part of my hesitation to follow up in a more vivid and decided way. However, other avenues must have opened since I have recently seen and purchased Moldovan wine in the U.S., though not yet in the U.K.

There were many trips from the UBS regional center to the countries behind the Iron Curtain to test out the viabilities of Bible societies in the surprisingly different state and church relationships. Next to the Soviet Union, there were Poland and the Baltic countries of Estonia, Latvia, and Lithuania. The decisive difference in these countries is that the Orthodox Church is *not* the majority church. Poland and Lithuania have a strong Roman Catholic presence. Latvia and Estonia are mostly Lutheran, with a Baptist diaspora further south. Hungary, Slovenia, Slovakia, and the Czech Republic owe their Roman Catholic dominance to their past in the pre-World War I Austro-Hungarian Empire. Serbia, Romania, and Bulgaria share an Orthodox majority. Among Protestant conservatives in the West, who share their deep philosophical, if not ideological, enmity against ungodly communism, there existed in those years the widespread assumption that Orthodox leaders must be linked to the Soviet KGB. In fact, because they were freely able to travel in the West to ecumenical conferences, they were seen to have held rank like a colonel in the KGB. I have heard the same from higher-ranking Baptist leaders. I have no direct or concrete knowledge of this situation; however, I do recall the pressure under which Lutheran church leaders in East Germany (GDR) had to sustain their limited freedom of worship left them by that communist regime. If Orthodox leaders would not have come to some symbiosis with the government, Stalin's pre-World War II suppression of the church might well have continued after the victory of World War II.

  The situation in Poland, and to a certain degree in Lithuania, was different. The Roman Catholic church took an openly critical stand against the Soviet surrogate regimes in Warsaw and Vilnius. A number of Roman Catholic martyrs are the proof of this position—a position firmly supported by the Vatican, especially under Pope John Paul II. That the Lutheran churches survived the post-World War II communist domination of Eastern Europe perhaps also could have had something to do with their leaders' relationships to their political regimes. But again, here I cannot condemn the attitudes. Lutheran church leaders since Hitler had to be mindful how they conducted their service in public. There is a fine line which separates those leaders who adjusted their service for the sake of freedom of worship for their people and those who saw in Hitler the

Messiah for Germany's post-World War I salvation. I doubt that in Orthodox circles behind the Iron Curtain Stalin ever had such messianic adoration.

My UBS contact with Poland and the Polish Bible Society in Warsaw was somewhat strained until my last visit in 1991. Barbara Narcinska hated Catholics but had a Roman Catholic bishop on her board. Barbara's husband, the Lutheran bishop in those days, had a low cooperative attitude with the regime and happily agreed to disagree with his wife. One time Barbara organized a trip for a UBS committee to Auschwitz. My friend Uli Fick and I were part of this excursion. To excuse ourselves from it would have been worse. Uli said: "We must hold a steely cloak around us when we walk through this Nazi concentration camp." And that we did. Neither of us would have wanted to have missed this experience. Before Auschwitz our UBS group was exposed to the famous Black Madonna of Czestochowa, another of Barbara's idiosyncrasies. As much as I would have liked her to be exchanged for her able Polish German deputy from Breslau, Barbara survived my active position with the UBS.

Estonia is different from Poland. Its majority church is Lutheran. There are two ways to Tallinn, its capital: one, the official way, through Moscow with a formal visa; and the other through Helsinki by Russian ferry to Tallinn for a day. I adopted the latter option several times. Once, on the trip back to Helsinki in the dark with light rain, the inside common room of this Russian ferry entertained its customers with the TV series "Dallas" in English. Was this an early rethink of capitalism, the arch-enemy of the USSR?

Tallinn is a beautiful city—medieval with some Germanesque style. There were no major UBS problems to solve in Tallinn. Bible work in Estonia was competently supported by Esco Rentala, the general secretary of the Finnish Bible Society. After all, Finns and Estonians are cousins, not only by language but also by their distaste for their Russian neighbors. For a short time we hoped that an Estonian Bible Society would find its concrete home in the

Estonian National Library, almost finished by the time of my last visit. It was at this visit that I saw for the first time the Estonian national flag flying from the tower above Tallinn. On the evening of that day I preached in St. Nicolai, a former Lutheran and now Baptist church. I preached about our common childhood as God's children baptized into Gods family. A U.S. Estonian Baptist minister translated. After the service a lady came to me and, with an impish smile, explained in German that my translator had told the congregation that not all of God's children had joined God's family by child baptism. Well, that is part of the delicacies of the UBS service to all who believe.

Another time, when I was in Moscow, I took an overnight sleeper to Leningrad, later St. Petersburg, in order to open a Bible depot and bookstore. At the opening the Metropolitan of Leningrad was present—a promising sign for the future of a Bible Society in Russia. This opening fell at the time when Gorbachev had ordered the Red Army to retreat from Afghanistan. After dismissal from the non-victorious Red Army, many soldiers found employ in the Afghan Mafia, which usurped protection money from public stores. The UBS Bible store could not afford that kind of money, nor did it make money from selling Bibles to the black market, where Bibles commanded a price ten to fifteen times its official price. This was the situation when the UBS Bible import was still at its humble beginnings. It was not long until the Bible store closed.

It was then that I took an extra trip to Leningrad to explore with the Metropolitan what political future a Bible Society in Russia might have. The decision for the direction of this trip grew out of the rumor in Orthodox ecclesiastic circles that the Leningrad Metropolitan might be a choice of relieving the old and ailing Patriarch Pimen in Moscow. In preparation for our meeting, the Metropolitan, as was the official custom in those days, organized the English to Russian translation. The Metropolitan had grown up in Tallinn; his patronymic was Ridiger. The conversation was quite useful because whenever the English translation ran into confusion, the Metropolitan corrected the situation with a quick half-sentence in fluent German. From this visit I took home the understanding from him that there might not come any opposition to a Bible Society in Russia.

It was around that time that Bibles were requested in amounts greater than ever before. From deliveries of 10,000 they grew to 25,000 and 50,000. The Orthodox patriarchate in Moscow asked for import permits and received them. When the requests came to 100,000 and more per year, the Stuttgart Bible Press ran into financial challenges, especially because of the long lorry transport costs which had not been realistically calculated in the UBS regional budgets. The patriarchate agreed to take over the transport of Bibles from Stuttgart. I remember having seen two or three huge SoveTrans six-axle Mercedes lorries loading Bibles in Stuttgart. As they were not the latest models of their type, I asked how many kilometers their engines had clocked up. "Oh, well over one million kilometers" was the answer. "We try to look after these engines as best we can."

In the meantime the Bibles were stored in the patriarchate on both sides of the stairs, on landings, in offices, and in the basement. It was at that time that the patriarchate considered the UBS its most valued supporter of cash. Under Gorbachev, many churches and monasteries were returned to the church. It's my understanding that many builders received payment in Bibles in exchange for properly restoring these buildings.

When I saw this in the English version of the *Patriarchal Quarterly*, I knew what would be coming from self-righteous conservative evangelicals: a malicious accusation of mercenary collaboration with the enemy. And it did! Of course, this development also increased the need to come to some decision about a Bible Society in Russia, with sufficient storage space and offices in quarters far off in the provinces. The other pressing question was how the Bible could be printed in Russia.

To this Erwin Zimmermann had the right answers: If the UBS would provide state-of-the-art thin paper printing presses, as it had successfully negotiated for China, it would be just the question of which print production plant might be the most suitable. When Metropolitan Pitirim became aware of this possibility, he arranged for me a meeting with Kniga, the USSR umbrella organization for all print and publishing.

My meeting with Kniga officers in one of Moscow's main streets near Red Square was simply unique. My question was where and what would be a suitable print facility which the UBS could equip with up-to-date thin paper presses for the production of one-volume Bibles. There was no answer except to say, "We don't produce paper that thin." They revealed that at that time Bibles printed in Russia were produced in two volumes. My response: "But if UBS were to import this paper from Finland? What would be the price for which you could produce a Bible?" They responded, "We don't work this way!" This sort of transaction was handled by the time-tested barter system. You name the price you want to pay per Bible.

"Don't you calculate a price based on your costs at a once-installed free press and paper? What would be your cost in labor, equipment, maintenance, depreciation, set-asides for later replacements, etc.?" There was no answer but some discussion, after which I was shown wonderful, big, high gloss art books and miniature Pushkin or Goethe editions—all very adorable, but not what I wanted to know.

Then came this unexpected answer: "Of course all transactions are influenced by the economy of the time and the availability of raw materials. For example, right now, we could offer you the penultimate version of a MIG Fighter for $25,000!"

With such an offer I found myself in an impossible situation. I thanked the gentlemen for their time and hospitality, packed up some of the print mementos still in my cottage, and left. On leaving they offered to arrange a car to take me where I had to be next. I thanked them, but I wanted to walk for awhile. Their explanation for offering the car was this: "Normally we have to do this so that foreigners don't get lost in our streets." I extended my thanks, but insisted that I really wanted to walk.

And that was most interesting. In Red Square I saw a Hari Krishna group chanting—until the police maneuvered them softly off the premises. In downtown Moscow the afternoon sunshine lets people look happy and at their best. Eventually I ended up in Pitirim's publishing house. He was not surprised with the result of the conversation. "We are not yet where you are economically." I wondered what he might have meant by that. Pitirim, to whom the UBS and I owe so much, paved the way for the Russian Bible Society. I would not be surprised if he was of the opinion that money in the West was so plentiful that one could pull it from the shelves with forklifts.

Just about that time the Norwegian Bible Society had found in its archive a highly appreciated and much needed two-volume study Bible from before World War I. The Norwegian Bible Society offered 10,000 sets to the patriarchate with the understanding that some of them should be shared with the smaller churches. This gesture contributed greatly to the process of clearing the path to the acceptance of a Bible Society in Russia.

Also around this time the aged Patriarch Pimen I died, and the Metropolitan of Leningrad became Alexy II the fifteenth Patriarch of Moscow and All Russia, the primate of the Russian Orthodox Church. In my first and only meeting with Patriarch Alexy II he offered us a Bible society if I would help him get rid of the swarms of fanatic Protestant heretics who had flooded the country since the borders had become so porous. "These people lure my people away from their faith in Mother Russia." I explained that I wished I could, but such was the price of freedom! We parted. Alexy II was followed as patriarch by the former head of the foreign office of the patriarchate, Metropolitan Kirill of Smolensk and Kaliningrad.

Shortly after this farewell, Terje Hartberg came back to the regional center with the news that the Bible society in Russia had been officially created. After my retirement

Patriarch Alexy II had consecrated the first temporary Bible house in Moscow.

I had promised Dorothy that, when the Bible Society was an assured reality, I would look into my options for retirement. I had no doubt that I was ready for retirement. It was not the workload that had brought me to this point— I was pleased and a bit proud of the network of contacts which my competent staff of the regional center had woven in Eastern Europe, a network strong enough to make possible the rapid expansion of Bible work after my departure from the UBS. What had worn me down, physically and mentally, was all the time wasted in airport departure lounges, while my office desk was piled with correspondence and matters for advice and decision. By 1991 it was thirty years of frequent and widespread travelling, which triggered the idea of retirement. And when my EKD personnel record in Hanover revealed that I had completed thirty-eight years, entitling me to a full pension, the idea of retirement became a concrete reality.

On my birthday, 26 September 1991, the UBS chairman, Siegfried Meurer, and the staff of the UBS Region for Europe and the Near East (including North Africa) released me from my duties. During the farewell dinner much was made of how far the region had come in building and servicing an infrastructure for effective and lasting UBS Bible work, particularly throughout Eastern Europe and North Africa.

Farewell to a Hurried Life

Dorothy, whose long illness began to take its toll, had read that retirement after an intensive and busy life can unlock some shock reaction. A tested antidote would be a journey without responsibilities for meetings. Dorothy surprised me with the information that on 1 October 1991, the first official day of my retirement, we would meet friends from California and Sidlesham at 7:00 a.m. at Heathrow Airport for a flight to—of all destinations—Moscow and a river cruise on the Volga to St. Petersburg. This journey was simply fabulous, with time for museums, excursions, palaces, and cathedrals for which I never would have had the time during my previous duty travels. We returned to Chimes Cottage in Sidlesham ready for some rest and reflection, but most of all with the resolve that from now on we would have time for each other. Both of us needed this break—not least in order to learn from our new life how to come to terms with the death of our son Marc on 10 August 1989, at age 26.

Yes, Marc's death hit us hard and unexpectedly. We were all ready for a family reunion with Marc in the Luneburg Heath in Germany three days later. I had called Marc the evening before he left for a weekend of mountain climbing to wish him well, together with fatherly advice to be careful and, most of all, to tell him that his parents loved him.

The accident happened on a Saturday. Marc and a friend from Rendsburg in Schleswig-Holstein had left early in the morning. Marc was driving his VW. It was hot. They reached the Bruchhaeuser Steine near Olpe in the south Westphalia Sauerland by noon. The decision was to have a quick climb up the straight rocks before lunch—because Marc, the more experienced climber, wanted to tackle the rock in the then-current fashion without ropes. Tragically he slipped and fell to the bottom. Since then it is my understanding that climbing at this site without ropes has been prohibited.

His funeral followed in Sidlesham. His gravestone states "He brought us joy." After her death in 2003, Dorothy found her rest next to him in the shared grave.

On his last trip to Sidlesham prior to his death, Marc, a fully accredited naval architect, had helped me find a seaworthy sturdy boat and comfortable replacement for the aging Dutch Lee Board Botter boat, *Puetz*, which had served us well since 1974, first in the Baltic and then in Chichester Harbor and the Solent. Marc's choice for his old man was a Fisher 25 with wheelhouse, heating, galley, and GPS navigation. She was built near Sidlesham, named *Puetz II*, and was taken over on my birthday in 1992.

Perhaps because this beautiful boat was Marc's choice, she became, throughout many sails with friends and family, a true sailor's comfort. Had Marc lived, he would have been her skipper from her launch. He was more competent than I ever managed to be.

For Dorothy the death of Marc remained forever an open wound. Often I heard her mourning self-reproach: "I, his mother, could not save my own son." Perhaps this natural, logical, but unjustified toll contributed to her long illness and death in October 2003. Dorothy remained grateful that she could enjoy her baby grand piano. Her piano playing often refreshed Chimes Cottage in retirement. After her death, her piano has its home at St. Mary our Lady Church in Sidlesham, where it is played at concerts and services.

During the months prior to her death, our love for each other and our memories of our life together gave us the confidence and peace to face a future beyond death. This Dorothy confirmed in the summer of 2003, on the day her doctor advised that her end was near. With her quick comment and smile she said, "So, I will see Marc before you!"

A New Chapter

A big change began to take shape in the summer of 2004. After Marc's and Dorothy's deaths I still had to dissolve the Florin Family Trust in California. On the way I stopped in the Twin Cities in Minnesota for a reunion with old friends from South Africa and Geneva, among them my friends Ted and Betty Homdrom. During dinner, Ted extended an invitation from his daughter and grandson, Ev and Victor Hanson, for lunch the next day. According to Victor's report of that lunch, it was filled with much conversation and laughter. The result was my casual invitation to Ev to Sidlesham before her holiday entitlement would expire at year's end.

In December 2004 Ev came to Sidlesham for a week. I was in the middle of renovating the kitchen and selling my boat. Ev helped in all that needed more than two hands and, together with Rod the gardener, laid down the new kitchen floor. The only outing that week, except for one evening restaurant meal, was taking *Puetz II* for a trial run with interested buyers.

That Saturday afternoon we left Birdham Pool on a falling tide. It was overcast. *Puetz II* behaved beautifully even on autopilot to Easthead in Chichester Harbor. Amidst a lively discussion in the stern of the boat, she went aground on an unmarked sandbank. My reaction: general embarrassment and assurance that we couldn't run aground on that spot. Revving the engine back and forth on that spot produced no result. We were stuck. So what would happen next?

Catching Ev's eye, I could see she was planning on going into the water. I said: "It's mid-December and far too cold. You can't do that."

Her response was: "I have enough warm clothes along to put on afterwards. And I have the longest legs."

What could I say as she disappeared into the cabin to strip down as far as decently possible. She went in up to her waist, rocked the boat from below while the interested buyers rocked from above. No result! What next? A quick call from the ship-to-shore radio (never used before) reached the Coast Guard at Hayling Island Lifeboat Station. "Where are you? We know where that is. We'll be there in ten minutes." And they were! They assured us this was a new sand bank—and in three minutes we were free. Hearing my accent, the lifeboat crew asked where we were coming from and whether they could tow us somewhere. I replied that I was from Birdham Pool and that I had sailed these waters since 1978, so we were left to find our own way home.

It should have been easy, but of course it wasn't. With rising darkness and falling tide, I took a wrong turn. Our interested boat-buying clients saw the pale outline of a church port-side and enquired which one it was. I knew there could be no church there. A depth check showed less than two feet under the keel—high time to turn around. But where were we?

Fortunately our clients had just completed their Offshore Navigation Test. A quick check on chart and GPS revealed our problem. With four knots we could reach Birdham Pool lock—due to close at 10:00 p.m. We reached the lock at 9:45 p.m.—exactly the time predicted by our client—and tied up. This demanded some fortification from the boat bar.

Around 11:00 p.m. we stepped ashore and went our separate ways home. After such a debacle would my customers still be interested? Ev's assurance was simple: "They will buy the boat." And, as so many times later, she was right. Before the year was out, the funds were deposited in my account, and the boat was no longer mine.

As Ev was departing for Minnesota, I said she must return so we could explore beyond Manhood Peninsula. In April 2005 we went to Cornwall and Devon. In the autumn that year Ev showed me St. Paul (I'd mostly been familiar with Minneapolis prior to this time), her alma mater in Moorhead, and the beauty of the north shore of Lake Superior—not knowing then that our future daughter-in-law Annie was from Grand Marais. At a wonderful garden dinner above the Red River in Moorhead, I approached my old friend and colleague Ted, now on his way also to becoming my father-law, with these words in memory of our close affinity in the summer of 1944: "Ted, you didn't get me, and I didn't get you, but now I get your daughter!"

On 20 May 2006 we were married in the Chapel of the Cross at Luther Seminary in St. Paul, a short walk from Ev's parents' home on Fulham Street.

It was Ev's wish to honeymoon at a place where neither of us had been. My old dream to explore Santorini, one of Greece's western Mediterranean isles was such a place. We can highly recommend Santorini, including its wines that come from the grapes grown on the ground with no moisture but the morning dew.

Back in Sidlesham the village was introduced to Ev at a garden party at Chimes Cottage. An unforgettable feature was a welcome to Ev with the lovely old, but not stale, madrigals. It was one of the last Saturdays when our lawn was still green before the summer drought.

This garden grass, after suffering through some dry summers, has again become lush and green and serves as Ev's summer yoga and t'ai chi chih studio. Through these and other village activities, Ev has become warmly accepted in her new home.

Reflecting on the Past

After twenty-one years of retirement and now, having relived my active past, I am aware of omissions in my life. But why has God Almighty granted me an interesting career? Like to all "why" questions, I have no answer. But I know that in retirement much of what was hoped for has happened. Yes, I have read much. Yes, time has been made for family and friends. And yes, I have sailed much in my Fisher 25 *Puetz II*: Chichester Harbor, English south coast with Isle of Wight, France twice, and Belgium–Holland once—all without my preferred skipper Marc, but fortunately all without deadlines. And I, too, am grateful that I can keep alive the memory of my hero, Bishop George Kennedy Bell, by supporting the George Bell Institute at Chichester Cathedral.

There has been time to fill interregna and substitutions in the German Lutheran congregations of Bournemouth and Portsmouth, and not infrequently I help with services in St. Mary's Church of England parish church in Sidlesham.

By way of taking leave I would like to illustrate some of my big "why" questions with some memories which have crystalized in later years. During the war:

Why was I dispatched to regimental headquarters in Duisburg the morning our 88-battery was bombed and we had casualties?

Why was I not hit the last morning on the eastern bank of the Elbe River, with the Red Army only one village away, when a mortar shell exploded at arm's length on the frozen edge of my trench?

Why was I among the few who got across the Torgau Bridge just seconds before it was blown up?

Why were a buddy and I rescued once more from the Eastern Elbe River bank—this time by two American GIs of Patton's army, who picked us up from the already Red Army-occupied bank in a boat, rowed by two Dutchmen, liberated from their captivity?

And why had I survived Nazi Germany's end of total collapse in utter "innocence"—without lasting physical or mental defects?

Even in the rural tranquillity of my life in Sidlesham, West Sussex, I cannot find the answers—other than thanking my Heavenly Father for letting me continue my days in the bliss of my marriage to Ev. Through Ev I have been blessed with a new family in St. Paul, Minnesota. Ev's father, Ted—my friend (and now father-in-law)—her/our son, Victor, and our daughter-in-law, Annie, with our lovely grandchildren, Adeline and Marcus, are an irresistible magnet of love to pull us across the Atlantic regularly.

Whether it is in West Sussex or Minnesota, I know that after an unexpected and probably undeserved hectic career I now, by the grace of God, live a relatively tranquil and rewarding life in sometimes hectic retirement.

Appendix

Acronyms

AACB	American Association of Christian Broadcasters
AACC	All Africa Conference of Churches
ABC	American Broadcasting Corporation
ABS	American Bible Society
ABC	American Broadcasting Corporation
AFN	American Forces Network
AMEX	American Express
ARSP	African Research and Studies Program at Boston University
BBC	British Broadcasting Corporation
BOAC	British Overseas Airways Corporation
BU	Boston University
CBS	Central Broadcasting System
CentComm	Central Committee
CISA	Christian Institute of Southern Africa
CLF	Christian Literature Fund
CRDS	Colgate Rochester Divinity School
CWM	Commission for World Mission
CWME	Commission for World Mission and Evangelism
CWS	Church World Service
DKP	German Communist Party
DM	Deutsche Mark (German Marks—West Germany's and Germany's official currency, 1948-2002)

EAGWM	Evangelische Arbeits Gemeinschaft fuer Welt Mission (EKD Protestant Mission Assistance)
EKD	Evangelical church in Germany— Evangelische Kirche in Deutschland
ELCSA	Evangelical Lutheran Church of South Africa
ELCSA-SER	Evangelical Lutheran Church in South Africa, South Eastern Region
EPD	Evangelische Pressedienst (Protestant Press Service)
EUREC	European Regional Executive Committee
DGMW	Deutsche Gessellschaft fuer Missionswissenschaft (German Society for Mission Studies)
HQ	Headquarters
ICCO	Interchurch Organization for Development Co-operation
KGB	Komitet gosudarstvennoy bezopasnosti (Committee for State Security)
LARACC	Latin American Regional Association for Christian Communication
LCA	Lutheran Church in America
LWF	Lutheran World Federation
LWF CWM	LWF Church World Mission
LWF WS	LWF World Service
LWH	Luftwaffenhelfer (Air Force Helper— Hitler's Last Hope)
MSP	Minneapolis/St. Paul
MIT	Massachusetts Institute of Technology
NBC	National Broadcasting Corporation
NBS	Norwegian Bible Society
NCC USA	National Council of Churches of the USA
NCRV	Nederlandse Christelijke Radio Vereniging/ (Dutch Christian Radio Association)
NECC	Near East Council of Churches
NEST	Near East School of Theology
NWICO	New World Information and Communication Order
PACC	Pacific Association of Christian Broadcasters

PBS	Public Broadcasting System
PCWM	Protestant Cooperative for World Mission
POW	Prisoner of War
PWMD	Protestant World Mission in Deutschland
RC	Roman Catholic
RVOG	Radio Voice of the Gospel
SACC	South African Council of Churches
SOAS	School of Oriental and African Studies, London University
SPD	Sozialdemokratische Partei Deutschlands (Social Democratic Party of Germany)
Spro-cas	Study Project of Christianity in Apartheid Society
TTEP	Theological Teachers Exchange Programme
UBS	United Bible Societies
UNFAO	United Nations Food and Agriculture Administration
UNESCO	United Nations Educational, Scientific and Cultural Organization
UNO	United Nations Organisation
VEM	Vereinigte Evangelische Mission
WACB	World Association for Christian Broadcasting
WACC	World Association for Christian Communication
WCC	World Council of Churches
WCC CWME	WCC Commission for World Mission and Evangelism
WCC DICARWS	WCC Department of Inter Church Aid, Refugees and World Service

Chronology

	Personal	**Political**
1924		Soviet Union (USSR) recognized by British Empire
1928	Birth in Schwerte, Germany	
1929	Florin family move to Gutersloh, Germany, father's chaplaincy	
1933		Adolph Hitler appointed chancellor
1937	Florin family move to Wuppertal-Barmen, Rhenish Mission Seminary	
1939	Started Wilhelm Doerpfeld Gymnasium, Wuppertal Elberfeld	World War II started
1943	School destroyed by Allied bombing, evacuated to Gera, Thuringen	
1944	Luftwaffenhelfer draft to 88 Battery, father's death	
1945	Antiaircraft service Torgau, American POW (April-August), return home to Wuppertal	World War II ended
1946	Return to school at Gutersloh	
1948		Nationalist Party elected in South Africa
1949	Abitur, high school graduation	
1950	Heidelberg theology student	
1952	Gottingen and Muenster theology student, academic theology examination	
1954	WCC scholarship, Colgate Rochester Divinity School, New York	
1955	Curacy in Hagen, Germany	
1957	Marriage to Dorothy Wilder	
1957	Boston University Divinity School	

Year	Event	World Event
1960	Ph.D., return to Gutersloh, ordination	
1961	Assistant director of LWF CWM, Geneva	Berlin Wall erected
1963	Birth of son, Marc	
1964	LWF assignment in South Africa, ELCSA	Nelson Mandela imprisoned
1966	EKD PCWM, Hamburg, Germany	
1971	General Secretary, EKD PCWM, Hamburg, Germany	Jauary 25 Ugandan Idi Amin coup d'état against President Milton Obote
1976	General Secretary, World Association of Christian Communication, London	
1978	Purchased weekend house in Sidlesham, West Sussex, for sailing *Puetz* Dutch boat	
1986	Regional secretary, United Bible Societies	
1982	Move to Sildlesham	
1984	Visited South Africa for the first time since 1965, after being denied a visa for 19 years	
1985		Gorbachev elected general secretary by Politburo, Soviet Union
1989	Death of son, Marc	
1990		Nelson Mandela released from prison, Berlin Wall destroyed
		Gorbachev elected first executive president, Soviet Union
1991	Retirement, ordered *Puetz II* Fisher sail boat	Soviet Union collapsed and dissolved
1994		Nelson Mandela elected South African president, apartheid ended
2003	Death of spouse, Dorothy	
2006	Marriage to Ev Hanson	
2010	Birth of granddaughter, Adeline	
2012	Birth of grandson, Marcus	

Index

A
Addis Ababa 38
African Research and Studies Program 15, 106
Afrikaans Broeder Bond 41
Alexy II 96
Amin 57, 72
Apartheid 41, 108
Augusta Victoria Hospital 24
Awori 72, 73, 77

B
Beirut 54, 55, 56, 58, 59, 77
Bell 17, 65, 104
Berleburg 9
Bibelsheim 7
Bonhoeffer 17
Boston University 15, 16, 106
Brandt 18
Brennecke 23, 39
British Commonwealth 32
Brown 15
Buthelezi 44

C
Cameroon 37
Catholicos 59, 77, 78, 85, 86, 87
Commission for World Mission 22, 32, 63, 64, 106, 108
Confessing Church 8, 9, 46

D
Dar Es Salaam 30
Diaconia 43, 47, 49, 62
Dorothy 11, 15, 17, 20, 27, 28, 29, 35, 97, 98, 99, 100, 101
Durban 42, 43
Dutch Reformed Church 41, 42

E
Egypt 51, 77
Ehrenstrom 15, 17
Emmanuel 67
Erk 50
Ethiopia 31, 38, 59
Evanston 10

F
Fick 61, 62, 92
Fischer 60
Fosseus 33, 38
Frankfurt 18, 48, 49, 53, 68
Freytag 13
Fry 26, 27, 67
Fueter 79

G
Gallagher 68, 69
Geisendoerfer 56
Gensichen 54
Gestapo 8, 9
Girkhausen 34
Goering, Herman 9
Guetersloh 8, 9, 17, 18, 19, 21, 34, 45

H
Habib 77, 78
Hagen 12, 13
Hamburg 4, 5, 12, 13, 14, 15, 30, 41, 42, 45, 48, 50, 54, 55, 58, 60, 64, 66, 70, 72, 73, 77, 80
Hammarskjöld 25
Hanover 22
Hartberg 79, 88, 96
Heidelberg 10, 11, 30, 54
Hermannsburg 35

Hermelink 13
Hoffmann 40
Holy Mountain 9
Homdrom 35, 43, 44, 101
Hurley 42, 43

I

Ilia II 83, 84
Israel 24, 80

J

Jan Smuts Airport 35, 44
Jayaweera 67, 76
Jericho 24
Jimbashian 79, 85
Johannesburg 35, 40, 44, 50
Johnson 66, 67
Jordan 24, 34

K

Kaiser Wilhelm II 24
Kaiser Wilhelm Memorial Church 24
Kaliningrad 96
Kampala 56, 57, 58, 72
Kannenberg 72
Kastlund 25, 26
Kenya 31, 56
Khotse House 44
Kilimanjaro Mission Hospital 31
Kirill 96
Kirkens Noedhelp 25
Kishinev 87, 88, 89, 90
Kniga 95
Knutson 35
Krause 35
Kuerschner 55, 70

L

Lee 49, 68, 99
Lehmann-Habeck 52
Liebich 50
Lilje 22
Lislerud 35
Lohmann 18, 45, 48, 60
Lohse 54, 78
Luebeck 23, 25, 65

M

MacBride 68, 73, 74, 75, 76
Makumira 30, 31, 32

Malta 68, 69
Marc 3, 27, 30, 32, 34, 35, 98, 99, 100, 101, 104, 105
Mbiti 57
Melzer 48, 49
Meurer 62, 97
Meyer 23, 25, 33
Mississippi 52, 53
Moldova 87, 88, 89, 90
Moshi 25, 26, 30, 31
Mound Bayou 52, 53
Mwombeki 48

N

Nairobi 31, 38, 56, 57, 58, 72
National Party 36, 37
Naude 41, 42, 50
Nelson 35
New York 10, 15, 16, 21, 51, 52, 53, 54, 67
Newbigin 20
Nkrumah 16
Nyerere 16

O

Obote 57

P

Pakendorf 35, 39, 40, 41
Palestinian 24
Patriarch 83, 84, 93, 94, 96
Pedi 39
Pelkman 55
Petersen 32
Pfeffer 14, 15
Philippines 54, 55, 69
Pimen I 96
Pitirim 83, 95
Poser 60
Potter 64
Pretoria 35, 40, 41

R

Randall 41
Rasmussen 11, 14
Rentala 92
Rhenish Mission 8, 9, 12, 45
Rome 20, 51, 52, 61

S

Schaeffer 9
Schiller 22, 23, 26, 28
Sekhukuneland 39, 40
Smaadahl 61, 79
Sovik 6, 20, 21, 22, 23, 24, 26, 33
Special Branch 39, 42
St. Mark 18, 20
Steinsiek 12, 13, 18, 19

T

Tallinn 92, 93
Tanganyika 37
Tanzania 16, 25, 30, 48, 57, 68, 76
Thimme 21
Togo 37
Traber 67
Tuyll 60, 80

U

Uganda 55, 56, 57, 72
Umpumulo 35
Untunjambili 35
Uppsala 25, 59

V

Valle 79
Vellipotes 77
Viehweger 50, 51, 52
Volokolamsk 83

W

Waard 79, 84, 85
Warns 34
Weimar Republic 8
Westphalia 18, 60, 99
Wigglesworth 79
Wilhelm Doerpfeld Gymnasium 7, 77
Wilhelm, Kaiser II 24
Wille 56, 57, 58
Wuppertal 7, 8, 9, 12, 77

Y

Yerevan 84, 85, 86, 87, 89

Z

Zimmermann 79, 85, 88, 89, 94
Zurich 61

Index ◆ 113

114 ◆ From the Unexpected to Tranquility…